Hello!

This experience happened after the last edit of this book. I liked the character of this story and decided it would be an interesting way to start this book.

I've asked the Angels many times how successful this book might be. They have never given me an answer. However, they gave me something interesting to think about the other day. My wife bought a book on orchids many years ago. Since that time, I've usually had a blooming orchid plant in our house. I was shopping recently and decided it was a good time to get another orchid. I had done my shopping and was in the parking lot loading my bags into the car. Right when I was putting the orchid into the car I heard yelling. A guy several cars away was looking at me and had just yelled something like: "Is that (orchid) to keep you out of the dog house?" I do not remember the exact words he used but they were congenial and funny. I told him it was my wife's fault. She had to have a book on orchids many years ago and that started this.

His response was great. He said that his son had given him a book on beekeeping ten years ago. Then he said that they had harvested 750 pounds of honey this year. We wished each other a good day and went our separate ways. I have no idea who that guy was. A book had got me to buy many orchids over the years. That guy had got involved in beekeeping because of a book.

This was a way for the Angels to reminded me that a book can make a change in a person's life. The right words to the right person can be very powerful. The exact same words can be meaningless to a different person. This was one more time that the Angels were letting me know that they wanted this book and this book has a purpose.

PHOTOS!

I showed many people the icicle cross photo while working on this book. Most people showed a lot of interest in the photo and many asked how they could get a copy of the icicle cross photo. That gave me an idea. I published the book in this size so that I could include the following photo pages. The first two pages are of the icicle cross. One image is full frame and the other is cropped. These images are 8 by 10 inches and can to trimmed to fit a standard picture frame. The third page has smaller images and a bookmark. All these pages can be cut out of this book (carefully). The smaller images can be made into refrigerator type magnets. If you laminate the book mark, it could last for years. Enjoy!

My Life with Angels:
an Unexpected Journey
by Gary Dean Butzbach
MyLifeWithAngels.com

MY LIFE with ANGELS:
An Unexpected Journey

by

Gary Dean Butzbach

Angeli in caelum
(Angels in the Heavens)

I think everybody in my family pronounces Butzbach slightly different. The way I have always pronounced Butzbach is Butch-baugh. Thank you.

The Angels wanted this book organized a certain way and a particular print size. Because of these choices in organization, the book ended up with several blank pages. I made some drawings of the icicle cross and put these on several of the blank pages. The Angels liked this idea. I thought the drawings of the icicle cross would remind the reader that the icicle cross was a gift from an Angel. Please remember that everything in this book really happened. Sometimes reality can be much harder to believe than fiction.

· ISBN 978-0-578-53652-1

THANK YOU

I want to say "THANK YOU" here. First, to my dear wife, Stephanie. We have had many years together (46 plus) and I am grateful for all of those years. I'm hoping for many more. When I talked to her about this book, she offered me her complete support. Her advise was: "don't hold back." I have tried to do that and tell you a complete story of my experiences. I need to say thank you to my father-in-law, Fred. Besides being a wonderful and dear person, he offered his complete support to this book. That means a lot to me. Thanks, Dad. I need to say thanks to several friends who have showed great support for this project. Thank you.

I have had tremendous support from many, many Angels for this book. They told me from day one that the book had to be in my own words. This book is better because of the steering and support that Angels have given me. The icicle cross is a wonderful gift from them. I hope that I have met my Angels expectations for this book.

MY BOOK

Foreword

The Icicle Cross

Introduction

Terminology

The Beginning

Angels – What I Know

The Fallen Ones

My Experiences
 Red Rock at the Gravel Pit
 My Broken Neck
 Choose a Store?
 The Little Blue Luv Truck
 The Luv Truck and The Apple Spill
 The Luv Truck and The Snowstorm
 The Old Pontiac and The Truck Tire
 My Cup Spilled
 When A Tree Falls
 The Ladders
 Black Ice on Hollywood Road
 The ER Experience
 An Afterthought

Events
Papa and Tinkerbell
My Father

Free Will & Angels

The Soul

Prophecy

Fears, Forgiveness & Faith

Heaven

The End?

Why Me?

The Most Unusual Events
The "Heart"
The Visit

FOREWORD

This is a book about Angels. I have had close experiences with these incredible creations all my life. This is also a book I never thought I would write. Who am I to tell you about Angels? Yes, I have had a lifetime of direct experiences and communication with Angels. All this amounts to lots of information about Angels. But I have still asked myself countless times who am I to write about Angels? The answer that I have always gotten back is simple and direct: "Just write the book." I have been told that by people and by Angels. **Just write the book!** So here it is. My book about Angels.

Many people may find the experiences that I will tell you about hard to believe. I can understand that. But the reality of the situation is that everything – let me repeat – everything in this book actually took place. The fact that all these things happened is one of the reasons that it was so difficult to write. Many of the experiences I'll tell you about are extremely personal and deeply emotional. But they need to be part of the book and so they are.

The Angelic Realm is a vast place. It is much, much larger than the world that we live on. The number of Angels in this realm is also vast. The majority of my experiences are with Guardian Angels. I have also had encounters with many other types of Angels. My Guardian Angels have saved my life many times and those are only the times that I am aware of. Angels are here to help us. I will tell you what I've learned about allowing our Angels to help us more.

I have a little story to share with you. It goes like this. Two people are talking one day and the subject of Angels comes up. The first person says very definitively: "I don't believe in Angels. They don't exist!" The second person simply smiles back and says: "I don't think Angels need your or my permission to exist." I think this story does a good job at creating a nice perspective for the question of Angels.

Angels are very real and always around us. They are by each of us all of the time. This is a reality of our existence. We can deny this but it won't change anything. So with this said, here is my book: My Life With Angels: an Unexpected Journey.

P.S. Here is an answer to a common question I have been asked about Angels. The Angels that I usually see don't have wings. They can have wings but most don't.

The ICICLE CROSS

This is the story of the icicle cross. I was having trouble finding a beginning to this book that I liked. That section just was not coming together quite right. I had taken a different approach to the beginning before going to bed one night. It was February, 2018. We were having some warmer weather at that time. When I woke the next day, I got up and when to the kitchen like normal. I looked out the kitchen window and there was the icicle cross hanging there. The morning light was making the icicles glow. We rarely get icicles on that part of the eave. The cross was about 24 inches long and 16 inches wide. It was a perfect cross shape with 90-degree angles. You may call it a coincidence but I know the icicle cross did not happen by chance. To me, it was confirmation of the new direction I was taking with the book and to help promotion of the book. The icicle cross lasted 3 days before it melted away. Many people like to be doubters. Months later, my Angels said to call it: **A doubter's cross.** They said **It's to make doubters doubt their doubting.** People that have tried to explain the icicle cross in some "rational" way but have never come up with a really good answer to explain how it came about.

Since I committed to writing this book, I have tried to be more open when talking about my experiences with Angels. People often have a very strong reaction to the photo of the icicle cross. The photo of the icicle cross has even caused some people to ask me when the book will be done. Just seeing the photo has made several people want to buy the book. One person that I showed the photo to stared at it for about a minute and then said they had a thousand questions that they wanted to ask me. Another person said they wished that we could talk all day after seeing the photo. Unfortunately, neither of us had all day to talk.

The icicle cross was created by an Angel. It is to be used as support for this book. Angels have sent me many little and some not so little messages such as: **Just write the book.** Look at the title of this book and remember what it says: "My Life with Angels: an Unexpected Journey." Everyone will have Angelic experiences during their life. You may not be aware of it but it is happening. This book is about my life and experiences. You are having your own life with your own Angels. Your experiences will be different than what mine are. How aware you are of your Angels is a question that only you can answer. My hope with this book is to increase peoples awareness of Angels.

The photo of the icicle cross was taken from inside my kitchen. I investigated the ratio of what is considered the "classical" cross commonly used in Christian churches. The icicle cross was extremely close in its actual dimensions to that ratio.

Each of us is at a different point of understanding on our journey. That means each of us will see the icicle cross from a different perspective. Some people simply see it as a strange icicle. Many see it as a sign or message. Others can see a divine quality in the icicle cross and can understand the power it represents. As I have said, we're at different places on our journeys so we will see things from different perspectives.

I'm sure there will be many doubters. They will doubt my experiences and all that I'm saying in this book. They will doubt the icicle cross photo. Doubters are sometimes doubters because they choose to take the easy way. It's easier to doubt things than to find your faith. Faith takes work. With faith, you must sometimes be willing to accept and believe things that don't have a "rational" answer. It is never easy to do this. There are times when you should doubt things. There are other times when you should not doubt. You must decide which is which for yourself. The icicle cross was very real. It is a truly wonderful gift from an Angel.

INTRODUCTION

Hi! My name is Gary. I have started this book many times but those starts just did not feel right for what I wanted to say. So this is what I came up with. I want this to be a conversation with you. I hope it comes across as a conversation. Especially the type of conversation that you might have with a friend while just sitting around and relaxing.

I'm just going to share my story with you. It is about what I have learned and been told by Angels. Yes, I said Angels. To start with, think of a baby. Have you ever seen a baby looking off into some direction, usually smiling? You glance at where the baby is looking and see nothing out of the ordinary. Chances are that the baby is actually seeing an Angel. I have seen this on many occasions. I have seen the Angel move and the baby follows the Angel's movements. Why babies can see Angels is a question that I can not answer. Nor can I answer why, as adults, most people can not see Angels. Well, my life has been a little different. Of course, I can't remember if I saw Angels as a baby but I do know that as long as I can remember I have been aware of Angels. I say aware because my ability to see and interact with Angels has changed much over my life. As I grew, so did my interactions with these remarkable creations. This includes "talking" to Angels. What I mean when I say "talking" is that I am having a non-vocal conversation with an Angel. The conversation has complete words and sentences but is not vocal. I have read about identical twins being able to communicate like this. I've had an identical twin tell me she can communicate with her twin this way. Angels can be very vocal. This can be loud. I have experienced that on a couple of occasions. The consequences of those times were often dramatic. What the Angels told me to do ended up saving my life.

Let me make it clear right now that there are both Good and bad Angels. When I just say Angels, I'll always be talking about the Good Angels. These are the Angels that are faithful to God and are here trying to help and protect us. The bad angels are the ones that were not faithful to God. These are the fallen ones that followed Lucifer and were expelled from Heaven. The fallen angels mean us harm. They will try to mislead and deceive us. They are often referred to as demons, devils, etc. When Lucifer and his gang were expelled from Heaven, they had their powers greatly reduced. That is a good thing for us. But the fallen ones can still cause us lots of trouble.

I will go into more details about Angels later including what I see, what they have said, and what they can do. I will talk about some of the many times they have saved me from harm including several times they have saved my very life. I've kept my Guardian Angels very busy. Most of my experiences have involved Guardian Angels. That should be obvious because your Guardian Angels are always by you. And yes, I mean always. At least one Guardian Angel will be by you all your life, from the moment you are born until the moment you die. Most people normally have two or three Guardian Angels by them. That can change in an instant. Many more Angels can be by them in that instant.

I will tell you how you can allow your Guardian Angels to help you more. I'll tell you how our free will can complicate things for our Guardian Angels. There are several other types of Angels. I have had interactions with some of these Angels and I'll tell you about that. Angels have even told me some about our souls. We, as in everybody, are on a journey. The physical existence we are in at this time is only one part in this grand adventure. Much more awaits us.

I know that some people will disagree with this book or at least parts of it. Some people will say I'm a nutcase or worse. Others will simply deny the existence of Angels. What I have to say to these people is this. Angels do not need anybody's permission to exist. Angels are very real. Angels are around you right now. You might as well accept it because Angels came before us, are here now and will be here after us.

This book is my story and experiences. Let me repeat, my story. This book is not intended to directly support or conflict with anyone's faith or belief system. Angels can assume whatever form they need so that they can fulfill their responsibilities. Everyone is going to have their own unique experience with their Angels. I have had experiences with Angels all my life and will speculate about why this may have happened.

If you would have asked me a few years ago if I ever thought I might be writing a book, I would have answered: "NO!" I had always wondered what it might be like to actually write a book since a writing class in high school. My wife has always been an avid reader but things changed when she got sick several years ago. She could no longer hold a book. Nor could she operate the controls on electronic book devices so that she could have books read to her. It was even difficult for her to handle the TV remote. So I offered to read to her if she could tolerate my pronunciation (and mispronunciation). We settled on less graphic murder mysteries. I often read to her before we went to sleep at night.

After the reading of many books, I began to think that I could maybe write a book. So I began to work on the plot, the characters and all the other details. I had developed a complete book in my head with all the characters and a complex plot. All I needed was some time to start writing it. That is when my Angels started saying that I should write about them. Even though I have dealt with Angels my entire life, that request took me by surprise. Yes, I have had a lot of experience with these Heavenly Creatures. Yes, Angels have saved my life many times. But to write a book about Angels? That is something I had never considered. But in many ways, I felt that I should try. So I talked to my wife about writing this book. She was willing to support my efforts. I started writing. And I start writing again. How do you write a book about Angels? I did some research but it really was not very helpful. So I started yet again. And again. These starts just did not feel "right".

So I was about to start this book yet again. I was sitting at the desk. Angels were on either side of me. I was frustrated because it just wasn't coming together so I uttered: "How do you write a book about Angels?" I got my answer. An Angel next to me said: **<u>You already know what to say. Just look to your heart!</u>** Well, how can you argue with that? Also, no pressure there. An Angel had just told me that the book was already in me. Of course, Angels are always right. So I took a different approach to the beginning of the book that night. The next morning, I got up and went to the kitchen like normal. Hanging from the eave outside the kitchen window was the icicle cross. That is the icicle cross I told you about earlier. The Angels, of course, were right. I kept that start and have just followed my thoughts since then. This book has a purpose. I may never know why the Angels wanted me to write this book. And that is perfectly fine. I just know that the Angels want this book. So here is the book.

I never intended to tell the world about all my Angelic experiences. I never had a need to share this. Until I started writing this book, few people in my entire life had any idea that I have had experiences with Angels. Not friends, not coworkers, not any family members. I had not even shared all of these experiences with my wife. I expected these experiences to pass away when I passed away. I had always kept this part of my life very private. Now with this book, all this is no longer private. The world will learn some of what I have been privileged to experience. Most of the people that I have known in my life will be surprised by this book. I was very good at <u>not</u> sharing my experiences with other people. Why should I have told people about any of this? I knew that a lot of the people that I worked with would have mocked me. Who needs that at work? Many of the friends I've had would not have been understanding either. So, I kept quiet until now. The Angels have something to say about all of this: **<u>Let them be surprised!</u>** I am now retired and can say what I want. People can take it or leave it. It won't hurt my feelings if somebody doesn't understand this. Remember, this is my story.

This book is a very, very challenging endeavor for me. I have to relive parts of my life to write this. That includes many of the most intense and emotional parts of my life. I knew that writing this book would be hard. So I asked the Angels why they wanted me to write this book now. Part of the answer that I got was: **You are strong enough now.** That answer did not make a lot of sense to me at that moment. I am now realizing part of what that answer means. I have kept so much of this information locked away inside me that writing this book has truly become 'an unexpected journey'.

I want to make you aware of some things about this book. Angels have always said that this book was be in my own words. However, Angels have been very insistent on certain design elements of this book. They wanted a certain paragraph style and font size, among a lot of other details about the book's design. This book may have been in my words, but I feel the book was definitely a collaboration between me and the Angels. I need to say thank you to the Angels for all of this. It has been a lot of work but a truly amazing part of my journey.

Please remember this as you read the book. I never asked to have any experiences with Angels. I do feel honored to have had so many experiences with Angels. All of this has definitely created unique challenges in my life. I am forever grateful to have been so privileged to experience all that I have and I would not ask to change anything. Our lives are full of things that we never asked for. Seeing Angels is just a part of my journey.

TERMINOLOGY

I was raised on a small family farm in southwestern lower Michigan. My parents went to a small country church that always used the word God to describe the Supreme Being. As such, I will be using the word God. If you use a different word instead of God please use that word. As stated previously, the word Angels will always reference only the Good Angels. Bad angels will be referenced as bad angels or fallen angels. There is a reason why I choose to call the bad angels either fallen angels or bad angels. If you use terms like devil, demon, etc., you are literally calling bad angels to you. If you use terms like fallen angels or bad angels, those terms do not attract them nearly as much. I like to keep the bad angels as far away from me as I can.

If you have not noticed yet, I am using a capital letter "A" when I am referring to the Good Angels or Angels in a general context but I am using a small letter "a" when I am referring to fallen angels or bad angels. There are two reasons for this. First, I have tremendous respect for Angels and all that they do for us so a capital "A" is a way that I show some of that respect. Second, using a small "a" helps make it clearer whether I'm talking about Good Angels or bad angels.

Any words or phrases that are directly quoted from an Angel are **<u>underlined and in boldface.</u>** I will use the terms direct or indirect to describe interactions with Angels. A direct encounter is when a person is actually seeing an Angel. Indirect encounters are what most people experience. This means you might be aware that an Angel is near and doing something but will not be seeing the Angel. Almost everyone will have indirect encounters with Angels. My encounters with Angels are both direct and indirect. I will often ask my Angels questions. Sometimes I will get answers. Other times I will only get facial expressions and sometimes nothing at all. There are other days when the Angels will be very talkative. Especially since I have started this book.

There are definitely times that all this information can be overwhelming. Seeing and communicating with Angels has been a daily event for most of my life. It's my norm and it would feel very strange if it ever changes. I am saying this because we often don't understand many things about our lives or why things end up the way the do. If my life was supposed to be like this so that I could write this book, then will all my experiences with Angels change after I finish this book? I hope I can still interact with Angels after the book but you never know. I guess I will just have to wait and see what happens.

I chose the word thread to describe a certain type of connection. Threads are thin and not very strong. Threads can be easily broken. These are the qualities that I need to use to describe a type of connection that we can have with Angels. A thread connection is a real connection but is weak and can be broken easily. These weak connections often can have a big influence in our lives. It is important that you understand what a thread connection is because bad angels like to use thread connections to get close to a person.

I will be using the word opening to describe a situation that we put ourselves into. An "opening" is an opportunity that can allow an Angel to have a greater influence with us. Many actions and some thoughts can create these openings. Openings can be used by any Angel (good or bad). Bad angels are always looking for openings. We can also close these openings. Openings almost always involve free will choices.

I needed names to describe certain types of Angels and other things in this book. I will explains all these terms as I use them later in the book.

THE BEGINNING

It was a coin toss, so to speak. I was born "sick." That is what my mother would tell me several times during my life. I do not remember her ever telling me exactly why I was sick. The doctors had only given me a 50/50 chance of living for the first two days of my life. If I made it those first days, my chances of living would improve each day. I was not premature or underweight. I was just "sick". I was put in an incubator (this was 1951). I spent weeks in the hospital before my parents could take me home.

My parents had a small family farm with mostly fruit trees. They were very good parents. They told me that the hospital bill from when I was born came to all the profit they had made on the farm that year. They never complained about it. My mother always said I was worth it. Just a family note: my brother, and only sibling, was almost 6 years old when I was born. He wanted a sister, not a brother. So, he had come up with a plan to give me away to our Aunt Martha. He had even made arrangements with Aunt Martha to come and get me the day I was to come home from the hospital. That didn't happen so my brother was stuck with a little brother. Recently, my brother told me that his real plan was to sell me to Aunt Martha for a quarter. Yes, 25 cents. If she did not want to pay, he would just give me to her.

I've often said that I have kept my Guardian Angels busy from the very first day of my life. In recent years, they have told me that was actually true. They have been saving my life from day one. Since I had been born sick, my father got a couple of cows so that I had fresh milk available. He kept the cows for many years. I can remember my father milking the cows. He would squirt the barn cats, intentionally missing their mouths so that they would have to lick themselves clean. The cats never complained. They were getting fresh milk! I always enjoyed that show. It's a nice memory.

I was always aware of entities around me. Remember, Angels can take any form that they need. I often had dreams about future events. If you are a somewhat shy kid, you quickly learn not to talk about things that only you are seeing. The Angels told me not to worry about that. They were here to help me. So, I got used to not talking about Angels to anyone. As I have already said, my parents had a small fruit farm. Most of the surrounding areas were also fruit farms. That made spring a wonderful time with all the fruit trees blooming. Maybe that is why I like flowers so much. To be in the middle of an orchard surrounded by hundreds of trees in full bloom is a special experience.

Our local school was actually a one-room schoolhouse that was built in the mid eighteen hundreds. It was made of bricks so it has always been called Brick School. The schoolhouse is still there today. Brick School had grades 1 through 6 and usually about 30 to 40 total students. Most years, there where only 2 or 3 other students in my grade.

Mr. Brink was the teacher when I was there. By the time I was in third grade he realized that I just wasn't doing well. I was struggling. My grades were C's, D's and even worse. Mr. Brink thought that repeating the third grade might help me. So, I repeated the third grade. Mr. Brink was an incredible teacher and would not tolerate bad behavior. I would have suffered a lot of social trauma for redoing a grade in other schools. But Mr. Brink would not allow that. My grades improved a lot after that. The school system had built a new elementary building by the time I was in the fifth grade. The old one and two room schools were closed then. I averaged A's and B's the rest of my school years and I even made the Principal's List a couple of times in high school.

Kids usually have a strong desire to fit in rather than be an outcast. It can be hard to try and fit in when you are seeing things so you end up not telling people about your encounters with Angels. The Angels always said that the day would come when I could tell people about my experiences. By high school, you are still trying to fit in. You are even beginning to think about your future.

The groups that I hung around with in high school were not exactly the "coolest" groups like the jocks or cheerleaders. I was in the more "brainy" and "artsy" groups. We did the Homecomings, Proms, Drama and other stuff like that. It was fun though. Many times my mother would let me take over the dining room table with projects. There were times that she even got involved with my projects. These are good memories. Very good memories. Towards my later years of high school, several people in my group started to get involved with seances and similar things. I went along with this stuff but did not take this stuff seriously. What I did not know was that I was creating an opening into myself that could let fallen angels influence me. Other events made this opening much wider. I would find out how wide this opening was soon enough. I started taking classes at the local college after high school. I really did not know what I wanted to be yet. The first year of college is mostly basis classes so I hoped to find a direction before the second year. I was dating more now and that was not helping me find my direction any sooner. There are times that we just need to live life more before we can find our direction.

I always had a creative side. I was able to take my first art class my senior year in high school. I really liked art. So, in college, I took several art classes and became very interested in that new technology: the computer. I liked programming and was very good at it. But I could not see myself sitting in a room programming code all day long. You need to remember that this was the early 1970's. We were programming using teletype machines, the kind that used rolls of paper to print on and did not have a video screen. I liked art - painting, drawing, sculpture - almost anything art. I even did a couple of neon sculptures for a class. But I couldn't see myself making a living in the art world. I, also, loved architecture but I didn't see a future in that. I still enjoy many creative things as hobbies. To this day, I still think about designing my dream house.

I was confused with religions at this time. There are still many things that I have not resolved about religions to this very day. I might have even called myself an atheist at that time. Because I was dating more and did not know what direction I wanted go in I was letting my grades slide. Remember how I talked about creating an opening in me? I would get together with a friend or two at night. We would just drive around and talk. Sometimes, we might get a snack at a local drive-in. I never was into drinking or drugs. Driving around was tame compared to the stuff that other people were doing.

One night, I was driving around with a friend, just shooting the breeze on some back road out in the country and probably driving around 55 mph. Suddenly, my friend becomes possessed! This is not a joke. A real possession is much more intense than any movie representation. They were talking in a totally different voice, very deep and very threatening. They were acting really scary. Their eyes went between shut and open but glazed over. At one point, their eyes seem to have a red glow. I was being told to join the "dark side" or else. I was scared. I mean really scared! I got my wits together. I asked: "Who are you?" The voice answered: "I am the devil and I can give you power! More power than you can imagine!" I could not believe it! I am talking to a devil? Then I answer: "No! No way!". The voice answered: "Okay – I will show you the greatness of your mistake!".

Right then, my friend began to open the car door and try to get out. I'm driving 55 mph and they are trying to get out of the car! It's hard to open up a car door at that speed because of the wind but they suddenly were strong enough to do it. I grabbed my friend's arm, pulling with all my might to keep them in the car while trying to keep control of the car and get it stopped. They were pulling hard. They had gotten one foot part out of the door by the time I got the car stopped. As soon as the car was stopped, my friend pulled their foot back into the car and closed the door. This had all happened so fast. It felt like an hour had passed but I knew it was only minutes. I was terrified, breathing fast, almost panting. I was wondering what would be next.

Then I found out what was next. My friend turned their head towards me and in a normal voice simply asked: "Why are we stopped?" They where okay and they did not seem to remember anything about what had just happened. I really did not know what to say. They were still looking at me. Just staring at me and wondering what was going on. They asked if I was okay. I finally said "yes". We were both safe now. I finally said that I had asked them a question several times. They had not answered so I stopped the car to see if there was something wrong. They shook their head no as they answered "no". Of course, then they asked what the question was. I didn't have a good answer. Finally I told them that I could not remember the question. It must not have been important. It was late so we decided to call it a night. I dropped them off at their house and headed home. All that I can think about as I'm driving home is how close that was to a disaster.

My friend didn't remember any of the possession experience. I knew that I should not tell them about it. So I have never told them anything about it nor do I ever intend to tell them about what happened that night. I had encountered a very strong demon that night and had a close call with a disaster. Way to close a call. I physically shook for the entire way home. I did not sleep well either. No surprise with that. All Angels have a presence around them. The presence of the demon was so dark, so empty, so cold, and so lifeless. That event has made it easier for me to sense the nearness of a bad angel. There have been a couple of lesser events with fallen angels since then. The possession event definitely caused me to refocus my attention to the Good Angels. Bad angels are here to do evil things.

I have had people question me about how I can know that I'm not being fooled by clever fallen angels? After you have experienced both good and bad types of Angels, it is very clear which type of Angel is present. The feeling that you get from the bad angels is so different than that of the Good Angels. Bad angels can not fake the energy around them. If you think that a possession in a movie is scary, it's nothing like a real encounter. A movie is a visual experience. An encounter with a strong demon has a bad energy that penetrates you to your very core. It's a terrible feeling.

Back to my college days. During this time, I had met someone very special. She was in high school and we began dating. I soon knew that she was the one for me. So I proposed and she accepted. I was still living at home then. I came home early one night. That wasn't normal for me. I told my parents that I wanted to talk to them. I had already dropped out of college and was working full time in a plastics factory. I told them I had asked Steph to marry me. My wife's name is Stephanie. We had a good talk that night. We got married with a simple civil ceremony soon after that. We had a plan. She would go to college, get her degree, and then work while I went back to college.

Things rarely work out as planned. Steph did get her Bachelors Degree and began working. She went on to get her Masters Degree. I had a few short term jobs but ended up working in a grocery store, first on a night crew stocking and later on in several other departments. I ended up being the Frozen Foods Manager in a couple of different stores. I have spent most of my working life in freezers. Just to let you know, I am retired now and don't miss the freezers at all.

With her degrees, my wife was able to make good money, often 3 or 4 times what I was making. She was over halfway to her Ph.D. when she got sick with Guillain Barre Syndrome (GBS). This is considered a rare disease where your immune system creates antibodies that attacks the myelin sheath (that is the insulation) on the nerves. The result of this is that the nerves misfire causing paralysis and pain. All the damage to the nerves is done in a few weeks. But the recovery period is measured in years. Depending on the actual amount of damage that is done to the myelin sheath, recovery can be from 5 years to 12 years or even more. During this time of being incapacitated, you can often develop many other complications that can affect recovery time. Unfortunately, she has had some serious complications. I'll talk more about these complications later. As of now, she has been ill for almost 11 years. She has many more years of recovery left to go yet. I have worked over 7 of these years. One of her complications has made it necessary for me to retire earlier that I had planned.

When you get hit with a situation like this, you just do not see how you are going to make it. Your income plummets. You are looking into a long tunnel for the recovery. You definitely feel overwhelmed. Well, our IRAs and 401Ks are long gone along with a small inheritance. We've restructured all our finances and with Medicare, Social Security Disability and recently Medicaid, we are still going. And I am glad that I have been here to take care of my dear wife Steph

Back to my experiences with Angels. My awareness of Angels was increasing by my early twenties. (I got married when I was 21.) I had become fascinated with the idea of being able to see the future. I was having dreams and sometimes visions of the future. These were always personal dreams and never worldly in nature. I focused on this a lot. The number of Angelic experiences I was having kept increasing as time went on. I had become much more comfortable with Angels constantly being around. Most people find even a little encounter with an Angel difficult to handle. I was actually expecting Angels to be around me all the time. Also, I was trying to listen to the Angels more.

I was still interested in the idea of "seeing" the future. About this time I began to have a recurring dream. The dream started in the fall of 1980 and lasted through January of 1981. The dream was short and the same. It had four parts to it. It always involved me hurting my neck. It somehow was connected to Kalamazoo, Michigan which is an hour drive from where we lived at that time. I was critically injured but okay and I would end up under the care of "true specialists." The only thing that made a little bit of sense with this dream was that I was in a car accident near Kalamazoo. But we were not going there at that time. I had this dream dozens of times during that period. How can a person be critically injured and still be perfectly fine? That does not happen normally. Then on February 6th, 1981, in the early afternoon, I found out what the dream meant. I fell and broke my neck. Before the day was over, all parts of the dream would come true. I kept my Guardian Angels very busy that day. I'll cover this full story later. After that day, my interest in knowing my future diminished greatly. Now I just accept each day as it comes and have learned to appreciate life so much more. That day, among several others that I will tell you about, could have easily been my last day. We need to plan for tomorrow but <u>always</u> - repeat – <u>always</u> live for today.

I hope this has given you enough background about me so that you understand my stories and experiences better. This book was never intended to be a biography. It's about sharing with you many of the things that Angels have shared with me. By talking about Angels with people, I'm able to understand more about what people what to know about Angels. These conversations can help me find better answers about my experiences. I don't have an answer for a lot of questions. But sometimes, I do have an answer. Either way, it usually ends up being an interesting conversation. Angels are real and amazing!

ANGELS: WHAT I KNOW

Many people have asked me: "What do I see when I see an Angel?" That is a very good question. An even better question would be: "What do I experience when I am by an Angel?" There are two parts to an Angelic experience. There is the appearance of an Angel. Then there is the energy or presence that surrounds Angels. I will try to describe both of these. Angels inhabit the Angelic Realm which Earth is a part of. The Angelic Realm is vast. There are many types of Angels in the Angelic Realm that are not here on Earth.

What characteristics do most Angels have? Most of the Angels I've encountered have some common qualities. Angels seem to have a very white, luminescent quality to their appearance. Most people will see Angels as being blindingly white in appearance. Even though Angels seems that bright, you can still look directly at them. I think a part of the blinding quality people experience from an Angel is because of the intense energy that surrounds an Angel. When an Angel makes its presence known, you can really feel the Angels energy. Angels can float about or stand. They can move about freely and very quickly. Angels can suddenly appear and just as quickly disappear. All the Angels that I have had experiences with have a human-like appearance. That means they have faces with ears, eyes, noses, and mouths. They have arms and hands. Their faces can be very expressive. I have seen Angels look happy and amused, serious and somber, befuddled and just staring intently. I particularly like it when Angels smile. Maybe it is because an Angel is smiling, but I enjoy seeing that.

I have never seen an Angel have expressions like anger or fear. Remember, I am talking exclusively about Good Angels now. The fallen angels are a completely different thing altogether. I do not believe that Angels have emotions like we do. However, I do believe that Angels have a level of empathy that is intensely strong. That can make an Angel appear to have emotions. I have seen Angels look like they were about to cry but have never actually seen an Angel cry. This was a situation where a person had just lost a loved one and was grieving. I've never seen an Angel show any expression that would look like anger or frustration.

As I have said before, my communication with Angels is normally all non-vocal. When I say I "talk" to an Angel, I mean this type of non-vocal communication. Angels rarely open their mouths during this type of "conversation" but often use their mouths in very expressive ways. Angels can make very powerful expressions. They can definitely vocalize if they need to. And that can be loud.

Angels usually hold their arms by their sides. However, they often use their hands and arms when gesturing. I've even seen Angles raise their arms and shout. That is quite an experience. An Angel's appearance depends on the type of Angel. Guardian Angels wear long robes with hoods and long sleeves. They all seem to have shoulder-length hair and the hoods down. Guardian Angels don't seem to have either a masculine or feminine character to them. An Angel's attire can range from various styles of robes to military style outfits much like you would expect an ancient Greek or Roman soldier might wear. The soldier type Angels definitely have a more masculine appearance.

What I need to explain here is why I am calling experiencing an Angel more than just seeing them. Angles are made up of what seems to be a type of energy. Even though most people feel blinded by the brightness they see with Angels, I think a major part of that reaction is caused by that person simultaneously experiencing the whiteness of the Angel along with the intensity of the energy that an Angel projects. You can feel the intense power of Angels full presence when they show themselves visually. Most Angels are in a muted mode as they go about their duties. An Angel in this mode does not have as strong a presence. The energy and power of Angels is unlike anything else I have ever experienced on Earth. If Angels are some type of matter, it is different than anything I have ever seen on Earth. Sometime in our future, somebody might be able to develop a device that can detect whatever material or energy that Angels are formed from. If that day comes, then a lot of doubters will have to rethink some of their doubts. We now trust invisible signals to quench our additive use of cell phones and usually get very frustrated when those invisible signals aren't available. Only the future will tell whether we all get to see Angels.

I want to talk a little more about an Angel's presence. You need to understand that the most powerful part of meeting an Angel is their energy field. I am repeating myself some here, but this is a very important part of an Angelic experience. The visual effect of an Angel in and of itself is very powerful. I think the experience of being engulfed by an Angel's energy field is what most people find overwhelming. Many historical records, including religious writings, document times when Angels have appeared before people. Almost always, the people are awed and overwhelmed by the very presence of Angels. The Angels will usually has to say things like: "Do not be afraid – I mean you no harm." People often drop to their knees and bow down to Angels. I think part of the reason that people act this way is not only are they awed and surprised by the appearance of Angels but they are overcome and engulfed by the energy emanating from the Angels. People are not used to experiencing any type of energy like this. Angels have an energy that is very intense. Hollywood might be able to represent an Angel's appearance. It is hard to imagine how Hollywood could represent the energy that an Angel emits. You know that you are in the presence of a great power. It's very hard to describe.

I have seen a person walk into a group of Angels and just stop. The person senses something. The energy from the Angels has made them stop and look around. They don't see anything out of the ordinary. Ultimately, they just go on their way. I usually have to smile to myself when I see this happen. A person has just walked into a group of Angels. They can feel that they have encountered something. They can not figure out what they have just experienced so they go on their way.

The names I have chose to use for some of the following Angels are based on what seems to be their primary functions or their appearance.

GUARDIAN ANGELS: A Guardian Angel will be with you from the moment you are born until the moment you die. There are a lot of Guardian Angels on Earth. The population of the world is estimated to be something like 7.5 billion people. Just out of curiosity, I asked my Angels how many Guardian Angels are on Earth on an average day. After a moment, they answered me. On an average day, the world has **25 to 30 billion** Guardian Angels and there are a lot more Guardian Angels that can come in an instant. Then, they reminded me that the Guardian Angel group is a large group of Angels but there are other groups of Angels that are far larger. When I say that there are a lot of Angels, I mean a LOT! I used to think that Angels are among us. Now I <u>know</u> that we are among the Angels

Guardian Angel seem to be about six feet tall. Their duties are to deal with God's wishes for us. Guardian Angels will usually use indirect means to help us. I assume any Angel can change their earthly form if they need to. Guardian Angels deal with people more than other Angels so they need to change their forms more often. An Angel can assume almost any form they need to accomplish their duties. Angels can even appear to be people just like us. You have likely encountered Angels that appear to be people and not known it. I have encountered Angels appearing to be people on many occasions. I've usually been able to sense their energy and realize that these "people" are really Angels. They are very good at seeming to be "people" when they need to be.

Sometimes, people might get a "feeling" or "intuition" about something. Intuition is often an Angel trying to tell you something. Angels will use dreams to communicate with us. These dreams normally stand out from most dreams. These dreams will have a different quality than your normal dreams. A dream that is influenced by an Angel will always have a very clear message. You may not understand what the dream means right away. You are likely to have that same dream repeatedly. Angels do not mince words. Any dream that an Angels gives you will usually be short and very direct in its message.

There are three levels within the Guardian Angel group. The levels represent the amount of power that an Angel has. Most Guardian Angels are at level one. Level two Angels are maybe one out of a hundred and have at least ten times the power of a level one Angel. There is a level three Guardian Angel which is rarer yet. A level three Angel probably has at least 1,000 times the power of a level one Angel. All Guardian Angels have the same appearance. You can tell the difference in their power when they let their presence be known. All Guardian Angels posses a lot of power regardless of what their level is.

Likewise, there are three levels of power among the fallen angels. Take note that even a level three fallen angel does not have the power to kill someone directly. A level three fallen angel is the only fallen angel with enough power to do a possession. I have encountered all three levels of Angels during my life, with both the Good Angels and the bad angels.

One of the things that Angels do is that they will influence the timing of an event. An example of this is the story that I tell (my spilled cup) about a drink getting knocked out of my hand and spilling on me. By doing that, the Angels got me to wait a moment after the traffic light had turned green. The fact that I waited a moment kept me from being broadsided by another car. That spill is an example of just one of the many times that Angels have acted to save my life. Guardian Angels have lots of things they can do to help protect us. I have heard of Angels moving people and even cars so that people would stay safe. Never underestimate the power that Good Angels possess.

These are some other Angels I have encountered.

MESSAGE ANGELS: This type of Angel is involved with delivering a special message to somebody or creating something that can be interpreted as a sign. Examples of Message Angels delivering a message often involve direct contact between the Angel and the people receiving the message. The experiences that the children of Fatima had with an Angel when they received several messages is an example of an encounter with a Message Angel. The Bible makes references to Angels delivering messages to the wise men and shepherds in the fields. The icicle cross is an example of a sign delivered by a Message Angel. I did not see an Angel put the icicle cross on my eave. But since then my Angels have confirmed that it was placed there by a Message Angel. Other signs that a Message Angel might deliver could include very temporary things such as a beam of sunlight breaking through the clouds to shine on something special. Message Angels can use a multitude of different ways to leave messages. There aren't many Message Angels. But their influence in the history of mankind has been significant, to put it mildly.

GUARD ANGELS: These are a type of Angel that I have only encountered in my life recently. My father-in-law had to go into the hospital for some surgery. While he was there, I took an 8 by 10 inch photo of the icicle cross to his hospital room. At that time, I'd only shown the photo to people but never given anyone a copy. The photo generated quite a few questions from hospital personnel. That did not really surprise me but what did surprise me was this. As soon as I put the photo on a shelf in his room, two Angels appeared, one standing on either side of the photo like they were guarding it. They had a military look to them. They just stood to either side of the photo completely motionless much like the guards do at Buckingham Palace in London. That is why I'm calling them Guard Angels.

This is not the end of the story. My father-in-law needed to spend several weeks in rehab after his hospital stay. I took the photo of the icicle cross to rehab and put it on top of a dresser in his room. Guess what? The Guard Angels were back. When he got out of rehab, I took the photo to his trailer and put it in the bedroom. The Guard Angels were there immediately and have been there ever since. In early 2019, my wife when to the ER and ended up being admitted to the hospital for two days. I took a framed photo of the icicle cross and put it in her hospital room. The photo generated a lot of interest from hospital personnel again. And more Guard Angels were back and on either side of the photo all the time the photo was at the hospital. So far, these are my only experiences with Guard Angels. I know some people will frame the icicle photos that are in the front part of this book. I don't know if you will get Guard Angels by the photos. Who knows? It just might happen.

THE SCHOLAR ANGELS: I have only encountered two of these Angels so far. When I first started this book, I would sit at the desk and type into the computer. These two Angels started appearing when I was working on the book. One Angel would be on each side of me whenever I was writing. I am calling them Scholar Angels because of the style of their robes. The robes tend to remind me of what professors might wear at a university ceremony. The robes that most Angels have are simple were the robes that the Scholar Angels have seem bigger with more details to them. These Angels would not say anything to me. They seemed to help guide my thoughts. It's not like they give me ideas or thoughts but rather they would "steer" me so that I could express those thoughts more clearly. It has been made abundantly clear to me since day one that this book is to be in my words. For some reason, the Scholar Angels moved their hands a lot. Their presence was always comforting. The Scholar Angels have helped make this a better book. I thank them for that.

ANGELS OF PASSAGE: This is harder to write about. There's no grim reaper nor any other "angel of death" that I am aware of. There is a special type of Angel that will come to carry a person's soul away when that person dies. I call this Angel the Angel of Passage. I've seen this Angel and I'll tell you about these times. All of these times were intense. Some were very, very intense.

The first time I saw an Angel of Passage was when I was in the hospital with my broken neck. I was in traction in a double occupancy room by the window. A new patient was brought in one day. The staff kept the curtain between us pulled out so I never saw what he looked like. Many medical people were coming and going all day long. Later in the evening, panic broke out. People were rushing into the room to his bed. They pulled the curtain completely closed. A nurse came by me and said sorry for all the commotion. I said it did not bother me and I asked if things were okay. The nurse never answered but had a very serious look on her face. Moments later I saw an Angel come into the room from the corner on my side of the room. That Angel was different from any other Angel I had ever encountered. It was shorter and squatter, almost like a robed person sitting on a stool might look. The Angel was still white but it had a very different quality to it. The activity around the other patient increased. Then his bed was wheeled out of the room. The Angel glided across the floor following the bed and people. The room seemed very quiet then.

What was different about this Angel was the energy and feeling that the Angel was emitting. The feeling was one of pure compassion. It is a very hard feeling to describe. Have you ever had a moment where the feeling of compassion is so overwhelming that it brings tears to your eyes? Take and amplify that feeling many times. That feeling from that Angel is enough to bring tears to my eyes even now. I was thinking that this Angel had something to do with a person dying. The next day, I found out. I asked my nurse about the other patient. I found out that he had died shortly after they had moved him out of the room.

I would see an Angel like this two more times. Another time that I was aware of an Angel of Passage was when my wife was at the ER. My wife was having issues but was not admitted to the hospital at that particular time. Suddenly, I sensed that an Angel of Passage was near. It felt like the Angel was only a couple of rooms away from us. I told my wife I thought that somebody was about to die. She asked me why and I told her about the nearness of an Angel of Passage. Soon there was a lot of commotion. At least one person was crying and started wailing a couple of rooms away from us. We asked a nurse later and my guess was right. Somebody had just died. I will talk about the other two times I saw an Angel of Passage in detail later in the book.

WARRIOR AND SOLDIER ANGELS: I chose to use these names because of the attire that these Angels seem to wear. Both types of these Angels have ancient military attire. This includes breastplates, helmets, and sometimes weapons. The main difference between these types of Angels is that they have different styles of military attire. I don't remember ever communicating with these types of Angels but I have seen a few of them up close. They are a little taller than the Guardian Angels, they always look serious and they always seem to be in groups. I saw a huge group of Soldier Angels moving across the sky at sunset once. They were at a distance but I could tell what they were. I do not have any idea why they were there but there were a lot of them. My best estimate of that mass gathering of Soldier Angels is that there had to be over half a million Angels there. Possibly more. It was quite breathtaking.

ARCHANGELS: Archangels are mentioned in many religious texts. These are the only Angels that have a name associated with them. They are very powerful and seem to have the duty of overseeing all the other Angels on Earth. An Archangel can visit Earth and interact with a person but that seems to be rare. Archangels travel with many other Angels around them. You might say that they have an entourage. A large entourage. If an Archangel needs to address you, they would do it directly to you and not through any other Angel or a person. An Archangel visiting someone would be quite an event with many other types of Angels present.

HUNTER ANGELS: I've never really encountered any Hunter Angels close up. I have been told about them and seen some at a distance. These are groups of Angels out there that are still trying to capture the fallen angels that roam among us. Here is where this gets more involved. We can unknowingly protect fallen angels from being captured and detained by the Hunter Angels. The way it seems to work is that if a fallen angel can connect with a person then that fallen angel can not be taken by the Hunter Angels. If a fallen angel doesn't have any connections to anyone, then the Hunter Angels can capture and detain that fallen angel. It seems to work this way because we have free will. If we use our free will and we make even a tiny connection to a fallen angel, that connection is enough to protect the fallen angel from being taken. Our free will has very great power in the Angelic Realm. This is why we should choose wisely when we use our free will. Poor decisions can create openings in us that can allow a lot of trouble for us. Even a thread of a connection to us can protect a fallen angel from the Hunter Angels.

There are other types of Angels that I don't have much information about. There is a type of Angel that is very similar to a Guardian Angel in appearance and power. I have seen such Angels among Guardian Angels. Maybe they are unassigned Guardian Angels. I'm still learning about Angels and still trying to understand what I have learned. Angels will never stop amazing me. The more I know, the more awed and amazed I become by Angels and of what awaits humanity

Angels can create some very unusual visual effects. One example would be what they can do with space. When you are in a room, there are walls, a ceiling and such. You can't just get up and walk through a wall. However, walls and ceilings are no obstacle to an Angel. What I have seen happen when there is a mass gathering is interesting. Angels can visually make walls, ceilings or anything else seem to disappear. Then you can see all the Angels that are there. If I were to walk towards a wall, that wall will still be there. Angels have done this in my kitchen on many occasions. That room is able to hold about twenty people if they were packed in tight. I've had some gatherings in the kitchen with thousands of Angels present. The walls just seem to disappear for these occasions. This is an interesting experience. Please note that this visual experience is a little disturbing at first and can take some getting used to.

If needed, Guardian Angels can appear to be people. You have likely encountered Angels this way at sometime in your life. They are able to blend right in with everyone else. They do this so well that I can have trouble picking them out of a crowd but I can still usually sense that they are Angels. When you get attuned to the energy that an Angel emits, it is hard for you not to be aware of that energy. However, Angels are very good at masking their energy when they need to appear as people. An Angel can appear to be any type of person. They can appear to be anything from young to old, tall to short, even friendly or threatening. Anything. They will be what they need to be. I can give you a couple of examples of this.

I wanted to take a copy of the icicle cross photo to put in my father-in-law's room when he was in the hospital. I needed a frame for the photo so I stopped at a store on the way to the hospital. All I wanted was a simple black frame. I took two sizes of the photo in the store with me to see how they will look in different frames. I found a frame that I liked and went to check out. There was one customer ahead of me. A woman got in line behind me as I was waiting. While I was being rung up, I dropped one of the photos and it fell on the floor behind me. The lady behind me was short and stooped over. She had a scarf over her head. I could not see her face because she was so stooped over. I reached down to get the photo and said "excuse me." The lady says to me: "Just write the book." I took my purchase and left the store. I had been sensing something about that "lady" but couldn't put my finger on what I was sensing. Then I knew what! That was an Angel! I knew it. I got to my car, got in and waited. I could see the register area in the store from where I was parked. Not only was there no "lady" insight anymore, but the cashier had left the front area by the register. I waited for several minutes but no "lady" came out of the store. I'd been involved with other stuff lately and had not been working on the book much. That was definitely a nudge from my Angels. I worked more on the book after that. A lot more.

This story was told to me by a friend. One of her close friends had a very unusual experience many years ago. Her friend was working in the city and would use a parking garage near where she worked. She had worked late. She got in the garage elevator to go to the level that her car was parked on. The elevator stopped before she got to her level and two shady looking guys got on the elevator with her. Recently, there had problems in the area. Two guys had been mugging and molesting women in area parking garages. Strangely enough, the two guys stayed at the far side of the elevator and didn't even look at her. The elevator gets to her garage level. When the door opened, two cops were there and they promptly arrested the two guys. The police asked her if the guys had tried to do anything to her and she told them no. Then the police asked the guys why they had not bother her. The guys had a very different answer. There had only been three people in that elevator according to the woman and the cops. The two guys told the cops they had stayed away from the woman because of the "two big guys standing by her." There were two Angels in the elevator protecting her from those guys. Without those "two big guys" in the elevator by her, she might have been molested. The cops and her never saw those two Angles. The Angels had done their job and protected her that day.

This story was to tell you that Angels can make their presence known selectively. I do not know whether the cashier in the store saw or heard the lady that was behind me that day. It doesn't matter. I got the message. **Just write the book!** I said I would write this book to my Angels which is the same as saying it to God. Remember, Angels act as God's instruments here on Earth.

Have you ever wondered why Angels look the way they do? Why is it that some Angels look like ancient soldiers and other Angels might have wings? Angels don't need wings. They can simply float anywhere they want to. What is it with the long robes and ancient armor? The best answer I have is that we have expectations. Think about when the first records about Angels were written? These writings are from a time when robes and ancient armor where the styles. The armor wasn't ancient then but you get the idea. If an Angel needs to make a direct appearance with a person, that Angel is most likely to have a successful encounter if the Angel appears in a form that the person might be able to accept. If Angels appeared looking like glowing orbs or other unexpected forms then chances are that a person would question whether the Angel is really an Angel. We have been given impressions of what to expect an Angel to look like from religious texts and stories. Angels will often use these expectations to make encounters with us work better. Outside of the Earth is a different story. Angels can be in their pure forms which seem to be energy. It would be very strange to have a bunch of Angels show up in unexpected shapes. An Angel appears looking like Elvis or a game show host? I do not think most people would buy that. You get the idea. Expectations can matter a lot!

I very often ask questions of my Angels. I might get an answer or not. An answer might come later. That later time could be hours, weeks or even many years later. Many times I have never got an answer. I was wondering how many Angels might exist. Not just on Earth but in total. So I asked. I wasn't expecting an answer. But I got an answer. Quite an answer. The answer the Angels gave to me is: **There are many, many more Angels than there is money on Earth**. I said there were a lot of Angels. That's a <u>LOT</u>!

There are special Angels that appear during Angelic gatherings and events. There can easily be a dozen or more different types of Angels present at these events. Some of Angels might speak but most are quiet. I don't know why these events happen but I have seen multitudes of Angels at some of these events. I've seen photos of crowds at events and estimates of how many people are present in those photos. Based on those estimates, there have been times when I've seen hundreds of thousands of Angels at some of these gatherings. These are unforgettable images!

I have noticed something around people that have bad attitudes. (These are people that are hypocrites, greedy, mean, judgmental, angry, hateful, etc.) People like this only have one Angel by them. Each of us will have one Angel with us all our life and most people usually have two or more Angels by them. But I never see more than one Angel by these people with bad attitudes. Having only one Angel does not make a person bad and there are times in our lives when we will only have one Angel by us. But bad people tend to always have just one Angel by them. I use a little more caution around a person that I do not know when I only see that they have a single Angel by them. At times, this caution has been extremely accurate.

I talk about how we are all on journeys. Many Angels are on their own journeys. I don't have details about what these journeys are like but I know that many Angels are on their own journeys. People have emotions including negative emotions like anger and hate. Angels have never experienced emotions, especially negative emotions. Angels are Angels and have always been Angels. It can be challenging for an Angel to understand a persons emotions. Angels do not need sleep. They do not get sick. They do not know what pain is. These things challenge an Angel's ability to help us. Angles are also tireless and always there for us. A part of many an Angel's journey is that they have a need to experience helping people. Somehow they benefit from this.

Angels are incredible!

Please understand that the next page was added after I thought I had fully edited this section. This addition definitely belongs in this part of the book.

First I need to talk about writing and publishing a book. If you are an established author or a celebrity, then agents or big publishers will talk to you. Otherwise, they will not even return an email saying: "Sorry – No thanks." Luckily, there are now some self publishing companies available. These companies are an important resource for people like me. But self publishing a book comes with a big learning curve. There are services that will walk you through the many steps in publishing for a fee. You should use some caution with these companies. They are in business to make money and don't care much about how well your book might do. I have wasted several hundred dollars with a couple of these companies. Some of these companies are very good while others are not. Just use caution. These companies want thousands of dollars for their services. Well, I'm on a fixed income and have limited resources. I had to take the most economical way that I could find. That meant that I had to do the vast amount of preparation work for this book myself. This is especially true when talking about editing. There is a lot of software now available for grammar checking and editing that does a very good job. Even with using this software, getting this book ready for publishing has taken many months.

I am now in what I hope is the last and final edit of this book. As I said earlier, I had the Scholar Angels by me much of the time I was writing. And I have already told you about how the Angels wanted many details of this book a certain way. However, the Angels always said that I was to use my words for the book. Until now. Some Angels have shown up by me when I am working on the book. They look similar to the Scholar Angels but are definitely different. There are always at least three and usually eight or more of these Angels when they are here. They <u>want</u> this book edited in a certain way. They will gather together as if they are conferring with each other while I work on the book. They haven't really "talked" to me but they have been very expressive about what they want changed. They have influenced my word choices and many other things about a sentence. They will stand there and will shake their heads back and forth saying "no" if they want me to change something. They will nod their heads if they approve of the changes I have made. They do this for only certain parts of the book. It could be only a word were other times it could be a sentence or an entire paragraph. I know that Angels act with purpose but this is the first time I have had Angels be this active with the actual writing of the book. I told the Angels that I would write this book and I intend to write the best book that I can. I always welcome any help I can get from my Angels. I haven't figured out what to call these Angels yet and I may never know why they want all these changes. But that is okay. I have a big list of things about Angels that I wonder about. And the list keeps growing.

Please note - if a Good Angel wants something, then a bad angel doesn't want that something and will do anything they can to interfere with it. I have told you that Angels want this book. I've encounter many "speed bumps" on the path to publishing. Some of those definitely involved bad angels. But the book is still going and will be published.

The Fallen Ones

When I say the fallen ones, understand that I'm referring to the bad angels or the fallen angels. These are the angels that sided with Lucifer against God and were expelled from Heaven. Most of these bad angels where captured and detained but some came to Earth and are serious trouble makers. They are often called devils, demons, etc. We are lucky that these angels had their powers greatly reduced when they were expelled from Heaven. I have been told the fallen ones had a **ten-fold** reduction in their powers. I am interpreting this as a 90 percent reduction in their powers. They could easily kill all of us if they still had their full powers yet. Now, they have to use trickery and deception to do harm us. The fallen ones have become expert at this. Terms like demons, devils, etc. act as a beacon to attract bad angels. That is why I choose to use terms like bad angels or the fallen angels. These terms don't seem to attract bad angels as much.

I have chosen to talk about the fallen angels separately from the Good Angels. I will tell you as much as I feel you need to know about bad angels but I do not intend to dwell on them. They would have us all dead if they could. You need to understand some about fallen angels so that you can protect yourself better from them. I have met fallen angels "face to face" and have no desire to give them any more consideration than I need to.

Bad angels are always looking for a way to harm us. They can take any shape they need to mislead us. As I've said, the energy they emit is totally different than the energy of Good Angels. The bad angels emit a coldness, a darkness, a feeling that people want to get away from. On the other hand, Good Angels emit a calming, a warming and even serene or peaceful feeling. Often, people have said that they feel engulfed by a great and wonderful power when Good Angels make their presence known. If you have at least a thread of faith connecting you to God, then there's a way to chase bad angels away. Say something like this: "In the name of God, bad spirits begone." The Good Angels will just stand there while the bad angels usually scatter. There are many more Good Angels than there are bad angels on Earth.

Everything gets much more complicated here because we have free will. Free will gives us the ability to choose between things, especially good or bad. We make certain choices that create opportunities for Angels to have more influence with us. I call these opportunities 'openings'. I talked some about these openings earlier. All our actions, our attitudes and even some thoughts that we have can create openings. Both Good Angels and bad angels can use these openings to influence us. Bad angels are always looking for an opportunity to connect with us. Any negative emotion such as hate, anger, malice, hypocrisy, etc. can create openings for bad angels to connect to us. Acts of violence or hate can create big openings for bad angels. Emotions like love, compassion, kindness, joy, etc. will create openings for the Good Angels. Positive acts let the Good Angels help us more. The choice is always ours.

I used to think that I had psychic experiences. These experiences usually involved premonitions and "feelings" about things. I have come to realize that I'm not psychic nor do I think that anyone is psychic. What I thought might be physic experiences was really having an Angel give me information. Both Good Angels and bad angels can do this. Good Angels are much better at this type of messaging than the bad angels. That doesn't mean that a bad angel can't use this technique to fool and mislead you. There are people that claim to be seers, good witches, psychics, etc. I've been told that what these people are experiencing is usually not in their best interest. Even if a bad angel can't get major control over you, they will still try to use any level of influence they can get to steer you away from good.

Some people say that they can channel information from an Angel for you. That is not how Good Angels normally work. YOUR Guardian Angel will be the one that sends you information. Not another person's Guardian Angel. Only your Guardian Angel. The Angel that was there at your birth, the Angel that will be with you all your life, and the Angel that will be at your side when you die. All my experiences say that your Guardian Angel is the Angel that will be communicating with you for your entire life.

Something that really bothers me are people that say they have a direct connection to an Archangel. They will say they can channel information to you from that Archangel. There are only a few Archangels. If an Archangel ever needs to tell you something, that Angel will be talking to you directly. An Archangel doesn't need to go through a person. Most people can't handle a direct face to face event with a Guardian Angel, let alone an Archangel like Micheal. Archangels have so much power in their presence that it pushes the boundaries of description. An Archangel is always accompanied by a host of many other Angels. I think that a lot of these people that say they can channel information for you are not getting their information from "good" sources. I would strongly suggest to beware of these people and especially what they tell you. Good Angels don't charge a fee or ask for a donation for their guidance.

If you find true faith within yourself, you will be able to find your own way. You don't need someone else telling you what your way is. Your path is already in you. The bad angels have become extremely clever. They have had time to practice their tools of deception. The fallen ones never have patience. The Good Angels always show patience. The only times my Angels have told me to do something NOW was when time mattered.

That **NOW!** ended up saving my life. Fallen angels have trouble acting patient for a few weeks yet alone a month or more. The Good Angels have patience that lasts a lifetime. A bad angel only wants to stay near someone if that person does negative things. Negative actions are protection for bad angels.

I know of a reverend that said he could give a person a "reading." I don't know if he was ever ordained but he always called himself a reverend. I know a person that went to him for a reading. That person says they were told things that the reverend could not have possibly known and were impressed with that information. They asked me how the reverend could have known such things. If you have not notice yet, I put this story in the fallen angel section. That is for a good reason. Any Angel, good or bad, can gather lots of information about you by observing you. Good Angels will only use this information to help you. Bad angels can funnel this information through someone like the reverend. The reverend does not need direct access to this personal information about you. All this information can be observed by a bad angel and given to you through someone like this reverend.

What is the harm with something like this? Potentially a LOT! Whenever you are dealing with bad angels, even if it seems like a harmless little thing, it is allowing a bad angel to have a connection to you. The fewer connections you have with bad angels, the better off you will be. The reverend probably believed that he was helping people. His intentions could have been good. If the reverend's services involved any connection to a bad angel then that would expose you to bad influences in your life. I'm not trying to tell you what to do here. That is entirely up to you. What I am saying is that you should be careful with things like these. These things can open you up to much more serious things later. A Guardian Angel will always tell you anything that you should know. I guess the bigger question here is whether you will be listening to that Angel. It's a very interesting idea to think that somebody can tell you what your future will be like. The actual reality of knowing what could be coming is not always what you would hope it could be. There are both good and bad things in our futures. It is often best that we face our future not knowing what it will bring. We should enjoy the good and deal with the bad as needed.

I have had direct and very intense encounters with fallen angels in my past. Some of that may have been decades ago but you never forget these things. I have seen them first hand. I know how intense and sly they can be. Faith and help from of my Guardian Angels saved me in those situations. I did not even know how strong the foundation of my faith was at that time. I am much more connected with my faith now and understand more about how much strength your faith can give you.

Any connection a bad angel can have to a person is very important to that angel. It offers that angel safety. Hunter Angels are always looking for fallen angels. They can only take and detain a fallen angel if that angel doesn't have any connection to a person. If that fallen angel has even a thread of connection to a person, that angel will be safe for that moment. The reason for this is that we have free will. Our free will is so powerful that it can allow us to unintentionally protect fallen angels. Hunter Angels must always respect our free will. Treads of connections are weak. These thread connections are very fragile and we can snap them at any time. Then fallen angels are vulnerable to capture. The only time that a bad angel will not be impatient is if they have a connection to a bad person. Bad people give fallen angels lots of safety. Fallen angels will stay by evil as long as they can. Fallen angels will always try to make sure that a person stays bad. In the world of bad angels, people that do bad things are their safety.

My Experiences

This section contains experiences that I have had where the intervention of Angels has changed the outcome. In most of these events, that intervention has saved me from injury and on several occasions death.

The Red Rock at the Gravel Pit

This event happened when I was in my very early teens. My mother had taken me over to a neighbor to play with some of their kids for the afternoon. The neighbor had a large family so there must have been about 5 of us in our group that day. I was one of the older kids in our bunch. We just headed off into the fields to "explore." We ended up at the edge of their property where there was a large gravel pit. It was not a pit but rather a big steep hill. They would take gravel from the bottom of the hill and more gravel would eventually slide down the face of the hill. It is dangerous to play at a gravel pit. We had been told to stay away from the gravel pit. You never know when more gravel will slide down the hillside. But we were kids. We were at the top of the hillside and worked our way around to the one side. From that point, I could see a large red rock on the face of the hillside. There it was, a piece of red granite. It probably weighed 30 pounds. That's not huge but we were just kids. I liked that rock and wanted to get it. But how?

Well, I had an idea. The hillside was fairly steep. I remembered that some of the orchards around the area, even a small orchard on my parent's farm, had been terraced so that you could plant rows of trees on them. Terracing? What if I took a stick and moved some gravel down to make a narrow ledge on the hill face. The rock was only about 30, maybe 35 feet out on the hillside. So I started doing that and it was working. The others helped me. Soon we were all out on that ledge and to the prized rock. I dug the red rock out and decided to get it to the edge of the hillside. The others kids were having fun and getting farther out on the hillside. I had got the rock to the edge and wanted to head back home with it but the others wanted to stay. I KNEW we needed to go so I said I'm going back with or without them. Reluctantly, the others came back to the edge of the hillside. As the last of the others got off the ledge we had made, a huge gravel slide came down the face of the hill. It wiped out all traces of our ledge and took gravel all the way to the bottom of the hill. If any of us would have been on that hillside yet, we would have been buried under tons of gravel. But we where all okay. We now had a rock to carry home. It was my rock so I ended up carrying it almost all the way back. We knew it had been a close call and we didn't talk a lot on the trip home.

My mother wasn't exactly happy with me when she picked me up. I was very dirty from handling the rock but she still let me take it home. That rock ended up setting along side the steps to the house for several decades. Not one of us kids ever talked about what had happened. We had been told to not play around the gravel pit. We didn't listen and almost paid a heavy price for it. But we were all okay. And we did stay away from the gravel pit after that. I knew there was a risk in going after that red rock. You are still a kid and just don't clearly see the consequences of your actions yet. Angels told me: **Get off the hillside**.   I had put all of us in danger. I am thankful that the Angels had warned me. I don't know how I would have felt if one of my friends had gotten hurt or worse. It left a lasting impression on me. All for a red rock. Kids!

My Broken Neck

I need to give you some background before I can explain how I broke my neck. The previous year I had bought a pair of "gravity boots." Gravity boots were padded shackle type devices that would allow you to hang upside down from a bar. You could do exercises with them but their main purpose was to let you stretch your back. I had a physical job so I made different attempts to stay healthy. Many of those attempts were short-lived. Some lasted longer. Gravity boots where later replaced by inversion tables which were easier to use and safer. The house we were living in at that time was old. It wasn't that charming fixed up type old. It was more the maintained and painted type old. Gravity boots needed a strong bar to hang from so I had installed one in a spare room upstairs. I used a steel pipe for the bar and chains to suspend it. I put big hooks into the ceiling and made sure that they were screwed into rafters. I had been using this set up for many months and everything was working fine. It was actually very relaxing to stretch out your back this way.

It was a Saturday afternoon, February 6, 1981. Our house had a long driveway and there had been a snow storm the previous night. I had shoveled about half the driveway. I was going to shovel the rest of the drive later that day. I was just relaxing so I decided to "hang" on the bar a while. That's when it happened. Like I said, the house was old. I was just hanging there, relaxing, upside down, and then I was on the floor. Apparently, the wood in the rafters had aged enough so that it let one of the wood hooks supporting the bar pull out. The bar was still hanging from one hook. I still had the gravity boots on. I had bit my tongue a little and could taste blood. That is when my neck began to hurt. The pain in my neck was getting worse by the second. I got the boots off and managed to get to our bed in the next room. My wife was working that afternoon. I used the phone next to the bed to call her. I told her I had fallen. I needed help. Come home. By the time I got the phone hung up, my neck was beginning to have spasms.

My neck was really hurting now. Lots of pain! I was getting more spasms in my neck. Intense spasms! I didn't know how to handle all this. I knew I was in big trouble. My Angels were by me. They told me: **Hold your neck as still as you can**. I needed to push up from the base of my head and try not to let my neck move. It was difficult to do but I did it. I had traumatized all the neck muscles. The pain was still getting worse. My Angels told me: **Go ahead and yell**. So I did. I yelled a lot. What did it matter? After several minutes of yelling, I stopped. My throat was getting sore from yelling and my wife would be home soon. I knew she was in a panic already and I didn't want to make it worse. I was still pushing up on my head. The spasms were getting less intense now.

I heard the door open. My wife was home. I yelled "upstairs" and she came to me. I had stopped pushing on my head at that point. I told her what had happened and she called an ambulance. The ambulance came and the paramedics looked me over. They did not think I was hurt that bad. I did not have any pain other than my neck and showed no sign of paralysis. They decided to put a soft foam collar around my neck, let me walk down the stairs and out in the snow to the ambulance. My wife asked about a backboard or something like that. Our stairs were old and steep and there was just a shovel-wide path down half the driveway. It would have been difficult for them to get me out of the house on a backboard. So they said that I would be okay with just the soft collar around my neck. The paramedics should have never handled me that way. They put me in great jeopardy. They would hear about this later from my wife.

It hurt a lot to move my head. I told the paramedics that I would be yelling when they put the soft collar on me. They put the collar on me and I YELLED! They did not expect it to hurt me that much. Then, I got out of bed and walked down the stairs. I got a coat over my shoulders and walked out to the ambulance. It hurt to change positions so I sat upright in the back of the ambulance. The ride to the hospital was painful. Every little bump in the ambulance hurt. I ended up walking into the ER. I was able to control myself enough not to yell when they had me lay down on a gurney. It was late afternoon by then. And a Saturday at that. My wife had driven to the hospital but wasn't by me. The doctor decided that I needed some x-rays and he talked to my wife. He said that he knew my neck was broken but he didn't think it was that bad. She asked him what was next. He said that I would be off work at least three months. The doctor wanted to send me home and have me come back Monday. The x-ray technicians would be back in on Monday. Then they could tell us more about the break. My wife asked if they could call a technician back in today. The doctor said it would take a while. She said either call a technician back in or transfer me to the neurology specialists at a hospital in Kalamazoo. The doctor reluctantly called a technician back in.

I would not find out about her conversation with that doctor until much later. In the meantime, I was just waiting and in pain. The spasms in my neck had lessened and I was very thankful for that. My neck just ached intensely now. The ER only had curtains separating the patient areas. Three people had come in and were taking on the other side of the curtain now. One person asks: "Where is the body?" Another person answers: "What body? He's alive. He walked in here." I'm hearing this and thinking this sounds bad. Very bad. I felt sorry for that person. Then, I see the three people peak around the curtain at ME! They were talking about ME! What have I gotten myself into?

That is when the ER went a little crazy. They got a lot of people in there and very gently moved me from the gurney to an aluminum board. A doctor began to explain that I would be taking a ride to a hospital in Kalamazoo to see some neurosurgeons there. A nurse was given the task of putting small sandbags all around my neck and head. Then she started wrapping my neck and head with gauze like a mummy. When she got to my eyes, I told her not to cover my eyes. I was awake and wanted to see what was going on. The nurse said she had her orders and started covering my eyes. I told her "no" again. The doctor was close but not paying attention to any of this. I told her to stop. She was ignoring me. So I grabbed her by the wrist, squeezed hard, and told her "I said no! Don't cover my eyes!" She's looking at me wide-eyed and surprised that I had grabbed her by the wrist. The doctor was looking at me now. The doctor looks at her and said: "Do what he wants." I let go of her wrist. She never said another word but did what I wanted. Just minutes earlier a doctor was ready to send me home for the weekend. Now they realized how serious my broken neck was and where taking every precaution that they could to protect me.

The trip to the Kalamazoo hospital was painful and uncomfortable. Ambulances ride rough to start with and being on an aluminum board magnifies every little bump. It doesn't help that they will not give you anything for pain when you have a spinal injury. That's actually for your own good. They need to know if a patient starts to have paralysis or other complications. The ambulance was now getting close to the hospital. It had been a very uncomfortable ride to say the least. The paramedics called the hospital, said that were about ten minutes away, and asked if they were ready for us. The first hospital had sent the x-rays of my neck ahead of us. The hospital answered with the following. They had got the x-rays and wanted to know why the ambulance was doing a "body transfer?" They had prepared a spot in the morgue for me. I could see the two paramedics looking at each other. Then the guy with the mike said: "Not only is the patient alive but he is listening to us right now. Can you please get ready for us." The answer that came back from the hospital was a weak "Okay."

It was now past midnight. They had called a neurologist in. I was being put in the neurology intensive care unit. That is when the fun began (sarcasm intended). They put me in traction. This starts with them shaving areas on each side of your head. Then the doctor screws these pointed rods into your skull which are part of a bracket. Next a cable connects to the bracket and goes to a pulley system that hangs over the edge of the bed. Finally, they put a 15-pound weight at the end of the cable. Most patients react very bad to having steel rods screwed into their skull so the doctor gets a lot of help. There were ten people holding me down. Two people on each leg and each arm. Two more people were holding my head. I would not have been able to move even if I wanted to. I knew this was going to hurt a lot but I was not going to fight. I was just going to let the doctor do his job. The doctor screwed the rods in my skull, he hooked up the cable, and put the weight on the end of the cable. I was now in traction. Then they gave me my first ever shot of morphine. That is also my last shot of morphine. I learned that morphine makes me sick. I stayed in the neurology intensive care unit until Monday. That's when I would get more x-rays. A lot more x-rays.

Monday came and I was moved to the x-ray department. They would use an x-ray machine that moves around to take what they called slice x-rays. They took slice x-rays for the top three vertebrae in my neck. These are cervical vertebra and commonly called C1, C2 and C3. The break was a compound fracture of C2. The projecting part on the back of a vertebra is called the spinal process. That was broke off but still lined up. The really serious break was on the front of C2. The front of C2 was broke completely across it but still lined up. A C2 break is commonly called a "hangman's fracture" because this is how they used to kill a person when they would hang them. This type of break is most often fatal. If a hangman's fracture is not fatal, then the person is usually paralyzed from the neck down.

An x-ray technician at the hospital told me later that they had never had a patient come in with this type of break and not be dead or paralyzed. I had been told that if any fragments of bone were by the breaks, I would go directly into surgery. They would cut pieces of bone off my hips and fuse C1, C2, and C3. I would be put in what is called a "halo" brace for 6 months to a year and I would need a lot of recovery time after that. I was praying that there were no bone fragments. Well, there were no bone fragments and the broken pieces of bone where all lined up. My neurosurgeon decided to be patient. I had already been through so much without having any complications. My doctor thought we should just wait. He figured luck was on my side. I wasn't talking much about Angels back then so I didn't tell him that there was more than luck involved. He said if my neck didn't heal by itself, we could always do surgery later.

I was in traction at the hospital for over a month. The steel rods in the skull really didn't hurt much. The sides of my head by the rods and my neck were sore for a week or two. After that, I really did not have a lot of pain. I was stuck in bed all that time with a 15-pound weight pulling on a cable to keep traction on my neck. The rods in my skull and the bracket created an unusual effect. Metal transmits sound much differently than bone does. This created an echo effect. This made it feel like I had a metal pail over my head. It took a few days to get used to that.

After a month, the x-rays were looking good so my doctor decided to take me out of traction and put me in a neck brace. The brace system had shoulder pads and support rods that came off of them. The rods connected to a strap system for the back of the head and a chin brace in front. The system was metal and plastic so you could take a shower or bath with it. The system was very good at immobilizing your head. A few days after being put in the neck brace, I was discharged from the hospital.

They never scheduled any therapy for me. The doctor said I could have rehab if I wanted it. He knew I did not need it. After being flat on my back in bed for over thirty days, I was walking the halls of the hospital the night after I was taken out of traction. I was not walking very gracefully that night and using the rails on the walls, but I was up and out of bed. My doctor knew that I would push myself because I wanted to get back to normal. All the neurologists and x-ray personnel at the hospital had told me that I had defied all the odds with my broken neck. It was several more months before I went back to work. I was off work a total of seven months. There was a lot of pain and discomfort over the next year or two while my neck adjusted and "normalized". But that is a minor price to pay for being alive.

I had just taught myself how to do the Rubik's Cube before breaking my neck. I had a lot of time to practice in the hospital. I was proficient at the Rubik's Cube by the time I came home. I'm out of practice now, but I can remember buzzing for a nurse more than once to come and rescue my Rubik's cube after I had dropped it. One last but very important thought about this experience. It was winter in Michigan when this happened. My dear wife came to visit me every day. Sometimes, she could ride with my parents. Other times, friends came to visit and they would bring her. She still worked full time and did this. The drive was over an hour each way in the winter. I told her she did not have to come every day but she insisted. I find it hard to describe how much this means to me even today, decades later. Thank you, Steph. My sweetie.

Choose a Store?

I have worked in several different grocery stores over the years. I worked in my first grocery store for over ten years. Then it was sold and then sold again. I stayed on but was finally laid off from there. It was a very big relief to leave that store because the business environment had changed much over the years and the store wasn't doing well. Ultimately, the store closed soon after that. I collected unemployment benefits for a few months while I was looking for a job. I needed a full time job with benefits, so that made the opportunities for jobs much more limited.

I had heard about a position available at a store that was not very far from where we lived, so I called the owner. The owner said he would be at the store all afternoon the next day. Just stop in and we could talk. I will call this the first store. Later that day, a friend of mine called me. He was the manager at a different store. He told me about another position at a store a little farther away. I'll call this the second store. I called the second store and was able to schedule an interview with the owner for the next morning. When I got to the morning interview, the owner had already checked me out through my friend. He offered me a full time position while I was there. He did not even ask me to fill out an employment application. The job would involve closing a couple of nights a week and would pay a little better than I expected from the first store. The owner said to go home, talk it over with my wife, and let him know in a day or two. I still intended to go to the first store that afternoon. The Angels kept telling me: **That it is a good offer. You should take it**. I knew that this was a better offer than I would get from the first store. So, I decided not to go to the afternoon appointment. I called the second store the next day and took that job.

A few months later, there was a robbery and shooting at the first store. A group of kids from the local high school had hatched a plan to rob and execute the night manager in at least three local grocery stores. If I had taken the job at the first store, I would have been closing several nights each week. I might have been working the night the kids shot the manager. The leader of the group was the gunman. He tied up the manager, took him into a cooler, and executed him. The store that I was working at was one of the other two stores on the kid's list. This was all premeditated. They caught the kids before they could do anything else. The leader ended up getting life in prison, and the others all got prison terms. A few years later, the widow of the manager that had been murdered at the other store started working where I was working. She had been pregnant with her third child at the time of his death. She was now happily remarried and going on with her life. It still scares my wife if I bring up this story, so I usually don't talk about it. One more time that my Angels steered me in the right direction.

The Little Blue Luv Truck

This is just a short note about a truck I had that was involved in a couple of very close calls with death. It was a used metallic blue Chevy Luv truck. It ran okay and I needed something to drive to work so I got it. It had a 4 cylinder diesel engine and got 38 miles to the gallon. It had a four-speed stick on the floor and definitely wasn't speedy. The engine would sound like it was going to blow up when you got the truck to 70 mph. But it kept going and going. It was always a little comic when I needed fuel. I would end up parked by the big rigs. The little blue truck looked very out of place next to those big trucks. Several times I had a trucker yell something like: "Hey, these are diesel pumps." I would always reply: "Thanks – I know", and I would fill up my little blue truck.

The Luv Truck and
The Apple Spill

I do not remember the exact month this happened but it was in the Fall because it was apple season. I was driving eastbound on I-94 with my wife in the little blue Luv truck. The highway is four lanes in this area and was moderately busy. I am in the right lane at this time. We get to a point where the road curves to the right. That limits how far ahead you can see. Traffic was slowing down quickly as I got to the curve. I had slowed down now. My Angels told me: **Get into the left lane** and I was able to do that. Then they said: **Get farther over to the left**. I did as they said. My truck ended up half off the road on the shoulder by the medium. My wife is asking: "What are you doing?" Traffic was completely stopped by now. She turned to look at the traffic to her right when there is a loud crash. Several large pieces of fiberglass and other debris are flying past her side of the truck. These were fender size pieces plus a lot of smaller stuff. The debris was just missing my truck.

I had been behind a tractor-trailer rig before switching lanes. Another truck didn't realize what was going on soon enough. That truck had just rear-ended the other truck's trailer. My truck and both of us would have been between those two trucks if I wouldn't have moved over. If I hadn't driven half off the inside lane, much of the debris from the truck's cab would have smashed into my truck with some breaking through the cab's rear window. But we were both okay. The front truck's trailer was loaded with scrap metal in steel bins. It was now 3 to 4 feet shorter than it had been. The cab of the second truck was essentially gone. The entire top of the cab was gone. Most of the fenders, grill and side panels were scattered all over the place. I think I saw some pieces of debris from the cab on top of the trailer ahead of it.

We got out of my truck, looking at the scene around us and trying to take in what had just happened. You could see the driver of the wrecked truck laying flat on top of the steering wheel. Strangely enough, after a minute or so, the driver moved, straightened up and was just sitting there looking around. There was nothing left of the cab above the dashboard! The driver is coming around and in another minute climbs out of what is left of his truck. He's okay! He's shaken up but he's okay. Then he starts saying: "My truck! My truck!" He just lived through this and he's worried about his truck. By now, a couple of police officers are here and walking around among us. The truck driver said he's okay but they still called an ambulance. And some tow trucks.

My wife and I were fine. My truck did not seem to be damaged in spite of the fact that there were several pieces of debris in the truck's bed now. If I had not done exactly what I was told by my Angels at that exact time, we definitely would have been accident casualties. If my Angels would not have told me to move farther towards the left, we still would have been hurt, possibly seriously, because of the flying debris. When you know your Angels, you do what you are told to do. It was their guidance that saved me and my wife that day.

The cause of the traffic mess that sunny Fall day was an apple spill. A truck was hauling bulk boxes of apples to a processor. One of the boxes break open and the apples spilled all over the road. Drivers thought it was okay to drive across the apple covered road. These cars slid off in every direction. When you are driving over apple sauce, it is quite slippery. Other than the wreck by us, there where no other wrecks and the driver of the truck was shook up but he was okay.   It was just a big apple sauce mess.

The Luv Truck and The Snowstorm

As you know by now, I live in Michigan. It was winter and winter brings snow to Michigan. In case you are not familiar with what a "whiteout" is, I'll explain. When you are having strong winds with a snowstorm, the wind can blow the snow around so much that you can not see anything around you. If you are driving in a whiteout, your visibility can become zero. Whiteouts are very dangerous and have caused many accidents.

Well, it was winter and we were getting a significant snowstorm with winds. My shift at work that day was to close the store. I would go to work in the afternoon and get done after midnight. I was worried about getting to work and much more worried about getting home later. Those worries would change soon enough. I had the little blue Luv truck at this time.

The wind was not blowing very hard when I started for work but it was snowing a lot. The road I took to work makes a long curve just south of town and gets near Lake Michigan at that curve. The closer to the lake I got, the stronger the wind got. The wind started to really gust just as I got to that curve. I was now in a total whiteout! I could not see anything outside of my truck! Not even the hood of my truck! I slowed way down. There was a high bluff to my right with Lake Michigan below that and oncoming traffic somewhere to the left of me. But I wasn't able to see any of these things at that moment.

Then, the snow let up some and all I could see was a car stopped directly ahead of me. I hit the brakes but still slid into the back of the car. The impact slid both of us ahead some and we ended up separated by about 15 feet. My truck had spun a little so that my driver's side was facing the rear of the car I had just hit. I caught my breath for a second or two. I wasn't hurt that I could see or feel and the impact wasn't really bad because the snow was so slippery. I was hoping the driver in the other car was okay. The snow was still blowing. The normal reaction after an accident is to get out of your vehicle, look at the damage and evaluate the situation.

I opened my door and started to get out. I had just got one foot out when an Angel tells me: **Get back in the truck.** I started to get back into the truck. Apparently I wasn't doing it fast enough. The Angel yells: **NOW!** I throw myself into that truck and just get the door yanked shut behind me when I get slammed on the passenger side by a big 4X4 truck. The impact pushes my truck back into the car I had just hit and spins me around. I ended up facing oncoming traffic. I am sitting in the truck trying to take in all of what has just happened. I think I am still okay. I don't feel pain anywhere. I was now facing oncoming traffic. I began to wonder what else might be coming towards me. I remember that I had passed a big front end loader. I am thinking that could be big trouble. Now I see flashing lights. It was a police car. The police car stopped short of our pile up. The snow and wind had started to lessen by now. The officer checked with all of us. We were okay but I requested an ambulance. I explained that I thought I was okay but my doctor had told me to always have my neck checked out if I was ever in a car accident. And this was definitely an accident. They called an ambulance and some tow trucks. While I sat in my truck waiting, I began to look around at the truck. The radio had been knocked out of the dash. The driver's window was gone. The rest of the inside of the truck didn't look to bad.

My wife had got a call from the paramedics and she met me at the ER. It turns out that my neck was okay– nothing new and I only had a couple of bruises. I was okay. The next day I got to see my truck. Or should I say what was left of my truck. Every bit of sheet metal was bent or crinkled. The bed was bowed up in the middle. All four quarter panels were crumpled. The roof was wrinkled and so were the doors. The tailgate was crumpled like an accordion. Because I did what my Angels had said, I was able to avoid being crushed between my truck and the car that I had hit. My Angels had done it again! I would have no more stories about the little blue Luv truck after this.

The Old Pontiac and The Truck Tire

Why should you listen to your Angels? Here is a good example. It's summer and very hot out. I needed to go to town. The route I would use was mostly side roads. Near town, I would get on I-94 (our local six-lane interstate) at Exit 27 and get off at Exit 28. I-94 crosses the Saint Joseph River between these two exits. I would only be on I-94 for one mile. I was driving an old black Pontiac with a dead air conditioner at that time. All the car windows were down and I was still hot. I got on I-94 and intended to stay in the right-hand lane since I would get off at the next exit. I ended up along side a semi-truck with it's trailer right next to my car.

All of a sudden, the Angels are yelling at me: **Close your window! Close your window!** I'm thinking "what"? They then yell: **NOW!** I hit the window switch and the window closes. Just as I get the window closed, one of the tires on the trailer next to my car disintegrates! Huge pieces of rubber are hitting my windshield. I thought the pieces were going to shatter the glass. It sounded like a hammer hitting the glass. Then another huge piece of tire hits my drivers window! I was sure the window was going to shatter but it didn't. This all happened so fast. I was at the next exit now and gladly got off the interstate.

If my window would have been down yet, a big chunk of that tire would have hit me in the head. Would I have survived a blow like that to the head? Would there have been an accident? I did not need answers to those questions. The Angels had saved me! Just a note: there where little pieces of that tire under my windshield wipers, stuck in the front grill, and more pieces stuck to my antennae. But strangely enough, no "new" dents to the old black Pontiac.

MY CUP SPILLED

I was working in a grocery store at this time. I ended up working in grocery stores most of my life. Today was one of the days that I was scheduled to close the store. I had done some errands earlier and grabbed a snack at a drive-thru. I was now ready to go to work. We lived in an older house in St. Joseph, Michigan at this time. The drive to work took about 25 minutes. All I had to do was zigzag through some side streets, get on Main St. and head south. Main St. was four lanes in this part of the city and divided by islands with planters and flowers.   There were traffic lights every few blocks to break up traffic so you could get onto Main St. from the side streets.

I would always catch Main St. at one of these traffic lights. The near side of Main St. was northbound. I needed to cross that and turn left onto the southbound side. So I started for work. I got to one of the traffic lights on Main St. and the light was red. I had some soda left in the cup from the drive-thru. The light turned green just as I was about to take a drink from the cup. Then WHAM! An Angel had knocked the drink out of my hand and into my lap!   I sat there a moment wondering: "why?" Then I looked up and saw "why." A car zoomed through the intersection in the northbound lanes on the red light. If I would have entered the intersection when my light had turned green, I would have been in a major accident. I waited to make sure things were clear now. I went back home to change my clothes and headed back towards work.

Later, I told my wife about what had happened. She explained that this type of accident was called a "T-bone" and even at slow speeds, it is often fatal. If the other car was going that fast (I estimated 40 mph), then it would have been over for me. I thanked my Angels again. I took a slightly different route to work after that.

When a Tree Falls-

When this event happened, I was living close enough to work so that it was only a ten-minute drive to and from work. The time was summer. I had an hour lunch break so I would normally come home for lunch. A big storm was just starting as I was heading back to work from my lunch break. It was beginning to rain and the winds were really getting intense. The normal way I used to go back to work was already blocked. A large branch had just broken off a tree and was in the road. So I had to turn around and take a different route. The rain was getting stronger and the wind was really gusting by now. I was going about 50 mph down the road when I see half of a huge old tree on the right side of the road start to fall. Half a tree was coming down just ahead of me! Half a Tree! If I slammed on the brakes, I would end up under that tree. There were deep ditches on the side of the road so going off the road wasn't an option. My Angels said **hit it** as in floor the gas pedal. I did. I veered to the left side of the road as far as I could and not go into the ditch. I had the gas to the floor.

I shot under the falling tree! I just made it through before the tree hit the road. My truck was hit by many branches as I went under the tree but I had made it. It was pouring rain by the time I got to work. A lot of employees were at the front of the store watching the storm rage on. I parked and simply walked into the store with the rain pouring down on me. They were looking at me wondering why I didn't seem to care that I was getting wet. Someone said: "It's bad out there." I said: "I know – I just drove through a tree." They looked at me. All I did was a nod. After the storm passed, I when out and looked at my truck. The front passenger side was a total mess. The headlight was smashed and passenger side mirror was gone. The front fender and passenger side of the bed were damaged. There was a big crease in the roof. The windshield had several cracks in it. Small branches were sticking out of the grill. There where a couple of larger branches in the truck bed. Insurance would cover the damage but it was quite an experience.

If I wouldn't have gunned it as my Angels said, I would have ended up under that tree. The road was closed for the rest of the day while the road department cleaned up the mess. When I was shooting through the tree, all I could see were branches and a lot of leaves. There is a scene in a movie about tornadoes where a truck shoots through a house. I know what it feels like to shoot through something like a tree now. I don't want to do anything like that again. It's not exciting. It's terrifying. My Angels saved me once again. A few seconds can be the difference between a disaster and safety.

The Ladders

This story is a little bit different than the other stories.

I was working in a grocery store as the frozen food manager when all these events happened. The door to the freezer was large and heavy. You can move a pallet in and out of a door that size. There was a row of pallet racks right next to one side of the freezer door. Pallet racks are the tall shelf systems that you can use a forklift to store pallets on. The store had two 10 feet tall ladders at that time. One of the ladders was made of wood and quite heavy. The other ladder was made mostly of fiberglass and much lighter. Well, management got the idea that these ladders should be stored at the end of the pallet rack right by the freezer door. The ladders were left just leaning against the end of pallet rack. I didn't think this was a safe or a good idea but my concerns were ignored. They insisted that <u>nothing</u> would happen. Right!

Nothing happened for a few weeks. Then one day it did. It was at the end of my shift and I had just closed the freezer door. I was standing a few feet from the door when WHAM! The wood ladder fell on me hitting the back of my head, my left shoulder and grazing the rest of my back as the ladder crashed to the floor. Another employee was nearby. They jumped back because the ladder makes such a loud bang as it hit the floor. They came over to me, asking me if I was okay. The ladder had hit me with a glancing blow. I knew I would be bruised and sore but I thought that I would be okay. If I would have been standing an inch or so closer to the freezer door, I'm sure I would have ended up seriously hurt or worse. It was late in the afternoon and all the top management were long gone. I had an invalid wife to get home to so I had the night manager write a report about what had happened.

I didn't sleep good that night. I was very sore. I get to work the next morning and find the ladders back exactly where they had been kept before. But now there were small elastic cords "holding" each ladder in place. I said I didn't think that the ladders should be there at all. I was told by management that the ladders were staying there. One person even said: "I should be more careful." Since I had a very nasty headache from the ladder hitting me the night before, I told management that I was going back home and I'd call them if I decided to go to the ER. I was quite sore so I just rested all day. I had taken a good hit from the ladder but what really got me was management's indifference. Sure. "I should be more careful." I went in the next day and the ladders were still there with their elastic cords. This actually worked for a couple of months. Then one day somebody did not put an elastic cord back after using a ladder. The wood ladder fell on me again. I did not get hit quite as hard this time. Management was already gone for the day again, so I left a detailed note for them about what had happened.

The next day that I worked, the ladders were back but someone had put a sign on the elastic cords reminding people to reattach the elastic cords after using the ladders. I didn't even address this with management. They did not care. Employees where getting hurt often at that store while management constantly complained about the high cost of their insurance. A few weeks later, a ladder fell on me again. It was the lighter ladder but it hit hard enough to almost knock me to the floor. Several people were there this time to see what had happened. I left the ladder on the floor were it had landed and put a note on it. The note said: "enough is enough." Do you want another workman's comp case? The next time I worked both ladders had been moved to a safer location were they could not fall. Management never asked me anything about this accident. Apparently they did not want to know if I was hurt.

You might wonder why my Angels would let the ladders even hit me. Each time before a ladder fell on me, the Angels had told me to step a little farther from the freezer door than where I would usually stand. Why didn't the Angels tell me to me move a few inches more so that I was completely out of the way? I wondered about that. But I also know that there are reasons why some things happen. This particular story came to mind when I was thinking about what to put in this book. That is when my Angels gave me an answer to my question about these events. The ladders had fell on me but without any permanent injury. An Angel told me that if the ladders would have still been kept by the freezer door after I had left that job, that somebody would have been hit by one of those ladders and **would have been crippled.** Yes, **Someone would have been crippled.** An Angel said those exact words. I still didn't feel good about getting hit by ladders <u>three times</u>. I did feel good about maybe keeping somebody else from being seriously injured. There are many times when faith is about trusting beyond our capability to understand it. Definitely!

Black Ice on Hollywood Road

Winter often brings snowy and icy road conditions. I would much rather deal with snowy roads over icy roads but we don't get a choice. Usually you can see the ice on the road and slow way down to deal with it. However, there are certain times when ice can form but it will not be glossy. This is commonly called black ice because you do not see it until you are on top of it. Black ice has caused many, many accidents.

One of the main roads in my area is Hollywood Road. Many people use this road to get to work so it has busy times early in the day and then later in the afternoon. I had a Mazda pickup at this time. I intended to go to town that afternoon and I would be using Hollywood Road to get there. It was early winter but it had not been snowing yet so the roads where in good driving condition. It's late afternoon and traffic was getting heavier. It had started to mist. Now the mist was rapidly freezing into black ice. Driving on ice is extremely dangerous because you can loose control of your vehicle in an instant. Ice was covering the road very quickly. In less than a minute, Hollywood Road had become iced covered. The road is now like a skating rink. I am trying to slow down while watching a car coming toward me in the other lane. That car is beginning to slide into my lane. I was going about 40 mph and I am guessing the oncoming car was doing about the same. My Angels said: **Don't slow down to fast.** This is the opposite of the normal reaction to brake slowly so that you maintain control of your vehicle. I did what the Angels said to do. That car is still sliding into my lane. I was hugging the shoulder and trying to avoid the oncoming car. The car was almost to my truck. I braced myself for the impact. The car is here! Somehow, the car is sliding past my truck and clips the corner of my rear bumper. The car passed my truck so close that I could have reached out and touched its outside mirror. That's way to close!

The car behind me was not so lucky. It got hit head on. Both cars spun around and slide to a stop. The cars behind them where sliding every which way as they stopped but none where crashing into each other. I had come safely to a stop now. I was mostly on the shoulder of the road. Another car had lost control and slide over a ditch on the other side of the road. There was a large furniture delivery truck stopped farther up the road. Hollywood Road was now blocked in both directions and was going to be blocked for a while. The delivery truck driver decides to turn the truck around. The truck immediately slides and gets stuck sideways in the middle of the road.

It was now quite a scene. A truck stuck sideways on the road ahead of me. A car sideways over a deep ditch. I still don't know how that car did that. And, of course, the collision behind me. Here I was, sitting in the middle of all this. I was fine and my truck was fine. Soon I could see emergency vehicle lights flashing. I could see police cars, tow trucks and a couple of ambulances. It had stopped misting but the damage was done. It was rush hour on Hollywood Road and I could see traffic backing up in both directions.

Eventually a police officer came up to my truck. He asked me what had happened. I told him. He asked if I was okay and I said yes. I asked about the collision behind me. He said that the two drivers in the wrecked cars seemed to be okay but shook up. They where going to take them to the hospital to be checked out. The officer stood there for a minute looking one way down the road and then the other way. He shook his head as he looked things over. He finally said that I was going to be stuck there for a while and then headed back towards his car. It was at least an hour or more before they got things under control and Hollywood Road open. At that point, I just turned around and headed back home. I did not need to go to town that bad anymore. The county road trucks where out in force salting and sanding by that time. The black ice caught everybody by surprise that day. Unfortunately, black ice often does that.

I inspected my truck when I got home. There was only a little scratch on the very edge of the back fender. However, the next day I noticed something stuck by the edge of the rear bumper. The bumper stuck out past the back of the fender by an inch or two. As I was looking at this, I realized that what I was seeing was black rubber. I began to pull at it. I ended up getting a strip of black rubber molding out from behind the bumper. The molding was from the side of the car that had slide past my truck. The truck bumper had peeled the molding off the car as it slide by my truck. The molding was about three feet long! I knew it had been a close call the day before but that showed me how close a call it really was. If I would have slowed my truck down just a little quicker, that car would have hit my truck in the front. That would have had a major accident. My Angels saved me from a wreck again.

The ER Experience

I've already told you that my wife has health issues. This event happened in July of 2015. Some of my wife's issues include a lot of pain. When you have nerves damaged through out your entire body, the nerves can generate a lot of signals to send to the brain and the brain tends to interpret these types of signals as pain. Sometimes extreme pain. My normal days off from work at this time where Thursday and Saturday. She had been feeling bad all day on Thursday. Neither of us got much sleep that night. I worked all day that Friday. She was feeling worse on Friday. She did not want to go to the ER. We did not get much sleep on Friday night. On Saturday afternoon, she decided she needed to go to the ER. Maybe they they could help her. We were both very exhausted by that point. Neither of us had got much usable sleep in three days. She was to weak for me to take her to the ER so I called 911 and had an ambulance come. The paramedics took her and I followed. It was late afternoon when we got to the ER. It was Saturday, July 4th.

I got her checked in. The doctor starts ordering different tests. Our family doctor worked at the hospital but not in the ER. He also had a private practice across the street from the hospital. The ER doctor ordered a pain shot of 50 mcg of fentynal. She had been given shots like this before and they had never caused any problems The shot did help some. We were waiting for test results to come back. I am very tired but hoping that they can do something to help my wife. If you have ever been to an ER, then you know that you can do a lot of waiting. And that is what we were doing. Finally, all of the test results come back. They couldn't find anything that would allow them to admit her. She was too weak to stand and in lots of pain but they needed something more to admit her. So the doctor says they were going to send her home. I am not happy with this because I don't even know how I will be able to get her into the house when we get home let alone make her feel better. But we're stuck with the doctor's decision. I had brought along her wheelchair. The nurse helps me get her into the wheelchair. The wheelchair was parked by the room's door. I'm sitting in a chair on the other side of the bed and wondering how I am going to get her home safely. The nurse has already disconnected all the monitoring wires. My wife still has the IV line in her arm. We are both exhausted. The nurse goes out and comes back with a shot. The doctor has ordered another fentynal shot. The nurse says he will get her discharges paper, gives my wife the shot and then leaves the room.

I look at the clock. It's exactly 6:23 PM. The Angels said: **Watch her.** So I did. The nurse has been gone only seconds. My wife makes a funny sound and her head goes back. I'm saying her name and getting no response. She not breathing! I'm up and out that door as quick as I can. I'm heading to the nurse's station. I get there. I'm yelling "I need help! She's not breathing!" I hurry back to the room. The doctor and nurse come quickly. The nurse has a shot with him. There is a short exchange of words between the

doctor and the nurse. It goes like this:
Nurse: "How much?"
Doctor: "All of it!"
Nurse: "How fast?"
Doctor: "As fast as you can!"

The nurse has the shot in her IV line and is giving it to her as fast as he can. The doctor explains that this shot is Narcan. Narcan instantly puts a person into withdrawal by reversing the effects of fentynal. The shot is in her. I look at the clock again. It's now 6:26 and 30 seconds. The doctor starts to say the following: "Come back. Stay with us. Don't go. Come back! Come back! Stay with us!" I am in the chair on the other side of the bed. My brain is racing. What's happening? I look at the clock again. It is now 6:28. My wife has not been breathing for five minutes and it's been 90 seconds since she was given the shot of Narcan.

I look back at my wife. That is when I see it and feel it. An Angel of Passage has entered the room in the corner behind my wife. The Angel is starting to move towards my wife. I want to jump over that bed. I want to get between my wife and that Angel so bad but I knew that it would not change anything. I don't think that I'm breathing at that moment. The Angel nears the back of my wife's wheelchair with its arms outstretched. I begin to see the glow of my wife's soul show at the back of the wheelchair. Just before the Angel touches the edge of her soul, my wife does this huge inhalation. I can hear that sound even today. She had started to breathe! The Angel pulls its arms back and slides backwards out of the room from where it come in. The doctor starts saying that she will probably be sick now because of the Narcan. They get one of those little vomit trays and she does throw up a little.

The ER is in total chaos now. Minutes ago they were sending her home. Now they are moving her into one of the big ER rooms. She was being wired back up. There must have been at least twenty people buzzing about doing things around us. My wife is now coming back but she thinks she is still dying. She is past the worst of this, I hope. Now my wife is trying to say goodbye to me. I feel completely numb from what I have just experienced. My wife is now saying things like "I'll miss you so much" and "I love you so much." I'm trying to tell her she will be okay but she "feels" like she is dying and just has to say these things to me. Hearing her say these things was making it even harder for me to deal with all this. She goes on like this for at least ten to fifteen minutes. The ER had called our doctor and he's here now. He's making arrangements to admit her. I can't believe what my wife has just went through. But my dear wife is still here! It was so. close. So very close. She had to have been only one or maybe two heartbeats away from dying. I am so grateful she is still here. I am so thankful that the Angels told me to keep watching her.

I never saw the other doctor or nurse again. They had left after this happened. My wife was admitted and spent four days in the hospital. Our doctor ran some type of heart test on her and didn't find anything wrong. I asked about other tests and was told she did not need them.

It would have been nice if this was just a close call but unfortunately it wasn't over for my wife yet. There have been complications after this ER event that affect her to this day. My wife was alive but very weak. She was discharged a few days later and I got her home okay. I expected her to be weak after an experience like what she had just been through. We had oxygen available at home. She needed to have more oxygen after this ER event. I felt the need to find out what happened in the ER that day. What had put my wife in such jeopardy? I tried to get her records. I was not having much luck. I got the hospital's patient advocate involved. Thanks to her, I got some records. But they were not complete. The records had been misfiled for some reason. What I got was most of the records for her stay but not the medical administrative record (mar). The mar details every order for any drugs used including the time the drugs were ordered, the amount of each drug, even the person and time that the drug was administered. After more digging, the patient advocate found the mar and got me a copy. Not only had my wife's records been misfiled to start with but the mar part from her records had been separated from the main records. The mar had been filed somewhere else.

The ER summary for her overdose experience was written up telling that she only got one shot of fentynal, not two shots. The mar shows that she got two shots and that the second shot was 100 mcg. That is twice the strength of the first shot. The second shot was given to her less than 90 minutes after the first shot. I wanted to talk to the head of the ER about this. It took weeks to arrange a meeting. The meeting would have the head of the ER, our doctor, the patient advocate and us. The day of the meeting, our doctor canceled at the last minute. We still had a meeting. It was a complete waste of time. The head of the ER would not really answer anything. He seemed to be mad that he even had to see us. Later, the patient advocate said she was sorry that the meeting had been such a disappointment. Fentynal can kill someone by suppressing a person's ability to breath. It is common for a person with Guillain Barre Syndrome (GBS) to have a compromised respiratory capacity. Many GBS patients need breathing support especially when they first get GBS. To give a large dose of a drug that suppresses a persons breathing to a GBS patient would be like giving a dose of blood thinner to a hemophilia patient. That is what the ER had done.

My wife had new issues after that ER visit. We were back at the ER in November. She was admitted, put into intensive care, and on a CPAP breathing machine for several days. It seems her carbon dioxide (CO_2) was extremely high. She gets sent home and was now scheduled for a sleep study to qualify her to get a CPAP machine. She does the sleep study but the technician doing the test does not finish it because he is running late.

There was a small procedure at the end of the study that he does not have time to do. So she is rescheduled for another complete sleep study several weeks later. When it is time for the next sleep study, my wife has gotten so weak that she can not do the study. She is back in the hospital again in April. This time, she is put in a regular room and put on a bi-pap. This helps a lot. Our doctor decides that she has hypercapnia. This is a condition where a person is not getting rid of enough CO_2 when they exhale. This can cause many problems. They scheduled her for yet another sleep study.

I knew my wife is so weak that she can not do another sleep study. So, I research hypercapnia myself. I was able to get the settings used for the bi-pap by the respiratory personal at the hospital. I ordered a bi-pap online, set the machine up and got my wife on the way to getting better, I hoped. When my doctor finds out what I have done, he yells at me. How can I know how to set the machine? I'm not qualified. I tell him what I have learned from sources online. Then I tell him I am using the same settings that the hospital's respiratory staff had used for my wife without a sleep study. He was still very mad. I am going to take the best care of my wife that I can, with or without, the help of professionals. They are just as human as we are. They are highly educated but they are not perfect. I respect medical people as being well educated. However, when the system is not working, I will do whatever I need to take care of my wife.

It is still an ongoing effort to find a way to improve my wife's situation. Recently, I have been able to start getting her to other doctors and specialists. I am hoping to find some more answers. It's also been over four years now since the ER event. I'm not about to give up on my wife. Never.

An Afterthought

Angels will often use timing changes to help us. Several of the experiences I just told you about involve timing. When a person learns to drive, you learn certain ways to deal with situations. These techniques tend to be reliable and are usually the safest ways to deal with events like snow or ice. My Angels have had to tell me to do several things that were not normal for certain situations so that I could avoid an accident.

I had a car pull out in front of me at an intersection one day. I had the right of way and they had a stop sign. At that instant, it didn't matter who had what. All that mattered was that I had to try to avoid an accident. My Angels told me to do this weird maneuver so I did what they said. I steered over to the oncoming lane, went half off the road onto the shoulder and turned sharply to the right. This got my car around the other car before that car could fully turn into the oncoming lane. If I had hit my breaks, I would have t-boned the other car on the driver's side. If I had turned away from the other car, I would have probably rolled over as I went into a deep water-filled ditch. Somehow the other driver had not seen my car coming. What the Angels said to do was right. We all ended up okay.

There have been other instances like this. Close calls but no accidents or injuries. I have learned to always be listening to my Angels. They have not let me down yet. You can question whether I am dealing with Good Angels or bad angels. That is always your choice. But I know what kind of Angels I'm dealing with. My Angels have saved me so many times that I can never consider doubting them. Fallen angels would have done me in a long time ago.

Events

The character of the following stories is different from the previous stories. They still involve Angels but in a different way. However, these stories are significant in the story of my life. These stories are part of the journey that got me to a point where I could write this book.

Papa and Tinkerbell

My grandparents died when I was young so I never got to really know them well. My wife's grandparents on her father's side were still alive. Over time I got to not only know them but got quite close to them. Their names were Fred and Helen but everybody in the world seemed to call them Papa and Tinkerbell. I don't know how Fred ended up being called Papa. I think it had to do with the fact that he was Fred Senior and his son was Fred Junior. By calling Fred Senior Papa, it would have helped you know which of the Freds someone was talking about. The Tinkerbell part is my wife's fault. The story is that when my wife was an infant, Helen would babysit Steph (my wife). Helen liked to call my wife Tinkerbell. Well, my wife thought that Helen was saying that her name was Tinkerbell. Soon enough, the name Tinkerbell stuck and everybody started calling Helen Tinkerbell.

Papa and Tinkerbell had a long life together but eventually, Helen got sick. She was in the hospital for a while and then came home. Papa had hired someone to help him take care of her because it was just to much for him. I went there to visit them one day and Papa was very upset. Tinkerbell kept saying, "I want to go home." She had been saying that for several days. She was frail and would just lay in bed with her eyes shut. But when she did talk, she would say: "I want to go home." Papa, of course, would tell her "you are home" over and over. But it was not changing anything. At that time, my wife was studying books dealing with death and dying for a class she was taking. I was picking up on some of what she was learning.

I wanted to visit Tinkerbell before I left there that day. I was able to see her alone in the bedroom. I stood along the side of the bed and gently took her hand in my hand. I knew what she meant when she was saying "I want to go home." Also, I knew what I should do. My Angels reassured me that what I was thinking was the right thing to do. So I told her who I was. Then I said that we all loved her and she can go home whenever she wants. I told her that we would all be okay including Papa. I said not to worry about us. It was okay for her to go home when she was ready. There was a short pause. Then she smiled but never opened her eyes. In her weak and frail state, she squeezed my hand so hard that it made my hand hurt. It was hard to believe that she had that much strength. When she let go of my hand, she still had a slight smile on her face. I told her that we all loved her and left after that.

She never asked to "go home" after that day. She passed away quietly a few days later. That was an incredibly hard thing for me to tell her that but I felt that I needed to do it for her. I could never tell Papa about this because he would have never understood. He would have hated me for saying that to her. This was about helping Tinkerbell. Papa wasn't at a place in his life that would have let him see it that way. He would have seen it as me trying to take her away from him. I'm not the type of person that cries easily but this was one of the hardest things I have had to do up to that time in my life. I cried all the way home that day. I told my wife about what I had done. She agreed that it was the right thing to do. To this very day, it is still one of the hardest things I've ever had to do. But there have been even harder things since then.

My Father

The time was Y2K. Yes, New Year's Eve 2000. My father was a heart patient and had gone into the local hospital that evening. He was having chest pains and my mother had called an ambulance. Fireworks were going off just as the ambulance got to the local hospital. That was on a Friday night. My father's heart doctor wanted him moved to the main hospital which had a cardiac section but there weren't any open beds at that time. My father was not doing very well. His heart was giving him serious problems. Monday came and they had space for him in the cardiac section at the other hospital. So he was scheduled for a transfer late that afternoon. My mother was not able to drive anymore because she had a stroke several years earlier. My dad had always said she had to go first because how could she make it without driving. Things rarely work out the way we want them to. I was at the hospital when the ambulance came to transfer my father. He was not responsive at that point. A friend had taken my mother home earlier. The plan was for me to pick up my mother and we would go to the main hospital. I had called my wife so that she knew what was going on. She was going to meet us at the hospital later. The ambulance took my father and I went to get my mother.

My parents were always dedicated to each other. They had met when they where in their teens. They got married (on February 14th) and worked on the farm together for all their lives. The important word here is "together." I was going through their things years later after they both were gone and realized that they had always carried the exact same photo in each of their wallets. The photo was of them when they were young with my mom sitting in the crotch of a small fruit tree and with my dad standing right next to her. They were happy when that photo was taken. They never had an easy life but the stayed together and always tried to be good people, especially to each other.

I picked up my mother and headed to the hospital. I knew she was very worried. We get to the hospital. As we are heading into the hospital, my cousin and this wife meet us at the door. They were there visiting somebody. My father's heart doctor saw them and knew we where related. He had asked them to wait for us and send us to the ER the moment we arrived. So we hurried to the ER. The heart doctor was waiting and steered us to a side area to talk. My father had "coded" during the transfer. That means his heart had stopped. The paramedics did get a pulse restored but they had a very difficult time doing that. Then the doctor asked us: "How heroic do you want me to be?" I will never forget those words. "How heroic do you want me to be?" I got my mother seated. She needed to sit down. I asked if my father was stable now. The answer was a weak "yes." I turned to my mother and said that we need to know some things. Are you okay with me asking some questions? She said yes. I really did not want to ask those questions. I was already guessing what the answers would be. But I knew we needed to hear those answers. So I started. "How bad was it?" Answer: "very bad – we almost didn't get him back." "What are the chances of brain damage?" Answer: "There is no way to tell for sure but from what I've seen before, the chances are great." "If he recovers, what would be involved? When might he come home?" Answer: "There are a lot of unknowns with things like this. I can only estimate that the best case situation is that he would be in the hospital at least six months, maybe a year and he might never be able to come home. I do not know if he will ever wake up again. Without life support, he would not be alive right now." I asked a few more questions. Then I asked the doctor if my mother and I could talk alone for a couple of minutes. The doctor said of course. He moved away but stayed within sight. He needed to know how to proceed with this. Those where some of the hardest questions I have ever had to ask anyone. But I knew that my mother was not up to asking anything at this time and we needed answers.

I was sitting down next to my mother now. We looked at each other I said: "You know how much Dad hates hospitals." We both knew it would be terrible for him to be away from her and her away from him. I said: "This has to be about what Dad would want. This can not be about what you or I want. We have to step outside of ourselves and do what Dad would want." Neither of us were crying. The blunt shock of the situation had us both numb. We knew what Dad would want and not want. My mother looked me in the eyes and said: "I think we know what we need to do." All I could say was "Yes." My mother was an incredibly strong woman. I turned to the doctor and he came back to us. My mother asked if we had time to call my brother and his wife to see if they could come. The doctor said yes. He explained that they would move my father to the cardiac unit. We could go there. When we were ready, life support would be turned off.

We had time to some talk before my brother and his wife got there. My mother said: "You know your father always said that I had to go first because I could not drive anymore." I told my mother: "We would make it work." We would make it work. We don't get to pick or choose how these things happened but I reiterated: "We would make it work." She believed me. My wife gets to the hospital. I told her what had happened and what was going to happen. We were waiting in the cardiac unit when my brother and his wife got there. I explained what was going on. My mother had asked the doctor how this would happen. He said that my father's heart was very weak. When they turn off the equipment that's keeping his heart going, it would only be a few minutes before his heart would stop. That would then be it. We gathered together in the room. My mother told the doctor she was ready. They flipped a couple of switches. The breathing equipment went silent. My father was breathing weak and very labored. It only took a minute or two for him to stop breathing. The equipment was turned off and silence filled the room.

That part of his journey was now over. There had been many Angels around me and my mother in the ER. The Angels were just standing about silently. The only time I remember the Angels doing something was when we had made the decision to stop life support. The moment we decided to stop life support, they all nodded several times. I took that as a confirmation about our decision. There where many Angels near us in the cardiac unit. As my father neared his last breath, I felt something. And then I was it. An Angel of Passage was entering the room from the far corner. The Angel's presence was flooding the room with an intense sensation of overwhelming compassion. That is the best description I have ever been able to come up with to explain this sensation. It's such an intense presence. The Angel of Passage possesses an unforgettable look to its face. The look has qualities of kindness, of mercy and, of course, compassion. The Angel of Passage approached my father, arms outstretched. At the moment of his very last breath, I saw his soul leave his body and the Angel gently cradle it, like a mother would cradle a newborn infant. The Angel looked down towards my father's soul and glided out of the room from were it had entered. At that moment, a nurse turned off the heart monitor and the room went silent. I stood there motionless. I had never seen a soul before.

After a moment or two of silence, we left the room and started to talk about what was next. My wife would go home. My brother and his wife would go back to their jobs. They had left work to come to the hospital. I would take my mother back to her house. We talked about many things on that ride. I said I would take the rest of the week off and help her make arrangements. I think that comforted her. I asked her if she would be okay alone that night. She said she would. That she had to get used to it because my father was gone now. I asked if she was hungry. The question was more about conversation than to really see if she was hungry. She said she might have some tomato soup. With a few crackers. See liked soup. Especially tomato soup. With crackers.

My mother lived until September 24, 2006 and we did make it work. I called her every day. My mother's name was Marie and her close friend's name was Marie. The friend would usually pick my mother up and they would meet other seniors at the local burger place for supper. The staff at the restaurant came to call them the 2 Maries. Also, they knew my mother's order by heart. I was taking to an appointment years later and I asked her if she wanted to stop at a burger place for a snack. Her answer was great. She said that it would be okay with her if she never saw another hamburger for the rest of her life. She still went out almost every night, the 2 Maries, to that burger place for years. It wasn't about the food. The food was fine. It was about the company and making her life work the best that she could. She was a great woman and friend. I learned a lot from my parents. I miss you both, Mom and Dad.

Free Will & Angels

Free will. We have it. It is a wonderful gift to us from God. It, also, causes us a lot of trouble and complicates our life in more ways than people realize. Cartoons have often represented free will as a little Angel on one shoulder and a little devil on the other shoulder. The devil is encouraging the person to do something wrong while the Angel is saying that you know better and should not do what you are contemplating. Free will is far more complicated that this representation. If life were only this simple.

Often, free will is about making choices between good and bad. But there is a lot more to it than just that. In it's most pure form, free will simply represents our ability to make a choice between two or more different things. It is also important to understand that we have the option of not choosing at all. When you use this definition, you can see that we are using free will all the time. The reason that it matters so much is that we are accumulating results of these decisions in our soul and will ultimately have to answer for all of these decisions. Choosing between good or bad are usually big choices and will matter more to our souls than smaller choices. Ultimately, every choice matters. Lots of little choices can add up. And the choices aren't necessarily about good or bad. Choices can be about something good or better and likewise something bad or worse. Choices can be about things that do not even seem to have a good or bad quality to them. These choices will usually reflect our true nature and are important. Then there is the matter of not making a choice. Not making a choice can be as important as making a choice. You need to understand that all of these choices really do matter to our souls after we die.

Many people may not understand some of the ways our free will can influence our lives. When we pray, we pray to God. God created Angels, in particular the Guardian Angels, as His instruments to carry out His wills for us. These wills come in two forms. The first form of God's wills I call absolute wills. Absolute wills are to be carried out by his Angels. They are absolute and they will happen. I call the second type of God's wills situational wills. These wills involve <u>our</u> free will. Situational wills are wills that God has granted but the Angels can only fulfill these after you have made the correct choice with our free will. I do not know how to tell whether a will is absolute or situational. I guess we will find that out later. This is why we need to know how important free will is. There are actually things that we can pray for and have God grant us but we can keep these things from being fulfilled because we make a wrong choice. Free will is powerful. Don't underestimate it's importance.

Guardian Angels can see what we are thinking but they are not normally allowed to act on these thoughts because we have free will. Plus, our thoughts are often jumbled so it can be difficult for Angels to see what our actual choice might be. However, once we state our choice, our Angels can act on it. So, if we speak our choice, even if we only mouth it as a whisper, the Angels can act upon it. This is important with situational wills. The decisions that we make in this physical part of our journey add up. They will matter greatly in the next part of our journey. I hope this has made you think more about your free will and how it affects you. Free will is a very great and powerful gift that we have been given. All to often, we seem to forget this.

The Soul

The soul. I always believed that we had souls. That was confirmed for me when I watched my father die. That was the first time I actually saw a soul. I almost saw a soul a second time. That was the ER overdose experience with my wife. I was very glad that I only saw the edge of her soul. If I would have seen all her soul, I would no longer have her here. Let me start with the shape of the soul. The soul seems has an ovoid shape (an ovoid is an egg like shape). The soul is about 9 inches wide by 6 inches high by 6 inches deep. The soul has a glowing and shimmering quality. The soul is white but is not that blinding white like Angels appear to be. The soul's color is more of a warm white. The soul has a pulsing quality that is very hard to explain but it definitely has this quality. To this very day, it is not easy for me to talk about seeing my father's soul leave his body.

Each of us has a soul. That is the essence of our life. Many people think that pets, especially dogs and cats, have souls. If animals have souls, then their souls are different than what a person's soul is like. I know that pets are often used by Angels to help us. That can make pets be very special and can endow our pets with special qualities. These special relationships between Angels and pets can make our pets be so much more than just pets. Angels are Angels. People are people. Pets are pets. We should always enjoy this special quality that our pets can have. This relationship is wonderful.

The soul is the core of your existence. The soul is what will go beyond your death and take you towards Heaven. There are people that say when we die, that is it. There is nothing beyond that. It is a person's right to think like this because you have free will. But this falls into the same area as denying the existence of a Supreme Being or Angels. You can say the Earth is flat but the Earth will still be round. You can deny God and His Angels but they will still be here. Blaise Pascal, (1623-1662) a famous French writer, mathematician, physicist, and theologian, wrote about why a "rational" person should believe in God. If you doubt God exists, maybe you should read Pascal's thoughts about this subject. A quote of his is: "We know the truth, not only by reason but also by the heart." The bottom line is that you have a soul.

What I understand about the soul is this: when you die, the soul leaves the body. It still carries with it the essence of who you were. That is all of your life experiences and memories. You will still have your free will. The soul is carried from your body by an Angel of Passage. The Angel of Passage takes your soul to the next part of your journey. I'm calling this place the Zone of Redress. When Angels were first telling me about this area, they did not offer me a name for it. They knew that I needed a name so they let me come up with a name. I researched words and ultimately settled on the Zone of Redress. The Angels definitely did some steering with this. The Angels stressed that the soul has to be **strengthened** and **balanced** before it leaves this place. I decided that Zone seemed to be the most accurate word to use. The next part was the Zone of what? The word had to mean **strengthened** and **balanced** plus much more. The word Redress has multiple meanings and seemed like a good choice. That is how I came up with the phrase Zone of Redress. The Zone of Redress is a huge place that can hold the souls of all of humanity at the same time. Each of us will be given our own unique pathway through the Zone of Redress. We have all had lives filled with different challenges and choices. The choices that we make now matter greatly in the Zone of Redress.

I look at the Zone of Redress as the gateway into Heaven. We will all be given the opportunity to be **strengthened** and **balanced.** When each of us finishes taking our own pathway through the Zone of Redress, we will be able to enter Heaven and be among all the Angels and so much more. However, we can refuse to take our pathway. We will still have free will and can refuse to do anything. The Angels have told me that if a soul were to enter Heaven before it's **strengthened** and **balanced,** that **the soul would be lost and would perish**. The impression that I have been given is that if we refuse to take the path we are offered in the Zone of Redress, our soul will ultimately be cast out and be **lost**. I don't know where that soul goes. I know that a soul will be **lost and parish** if it is cast out from the Zone of Redress. I don't think there is a way to enter the Zone of Redress again once a soul is cast out.

God wants to save all souls. God is more about love than anything else. God has created many paths for us to use to get into Heaven. It is entirely up to us to accept and take the path the we are offered. We are imperfect and God knows this. If we try to be good we will have an easier path to Heaven. If we are knowingly bad, our pathway will be harder. God has created many paths for us to use for His forgiveness. It all depends on what our life was as to the exact path we will be offered. As I said, God wants to save all souls. Saving souls is important to God.

I do not think that there is a place called Hell. I believe that really bad people will have paths through the Zone of Redress that we would probably describe as Hell. Some people have burdened their souls so much that the **strengthening** and **balancing** needed in the Zone of Redress could easily seem like Hell. The fact is, we can save ourselves. Our decisions on this earthly part of our journey matter more than most of us think. Our souls will be going through a metamorphosis in the Zone of Redress. We will leave there completely different from what we were when we entered there. If any of the glimpses I have had are any indication of what lies ahead, then our future is way beyond amazing.

Prophecy

Most major religious works talk about prophecies and the future. I always had a difficult time trying to understand how free will and prophecies can both coexist. Certain events have to happen in some sort of order for a prophecy to happen. Free will has no predictability and is constantly changing things. So how can these two different things exist at the same time. Then I came to the realize that both of these do exist without any conflicts. You just need to think about what prophecies are in a slightly different way.

People have free will. This is a fact. Free will allows you to make choices. Those choices can change the direction of things. These changes will not only influence your life but can easily influence other people's lives. So, the question becomes, how can a prophecy happen in the future with these changes happening all the time? The answer is easier than you think. A prophecy does not deal with timing as much as it deals with the order of events. As an example, to fulfill a prophecy, you will need a series of events to happen. Let's say there are five events that must happen for a prophecy to be fulfilled. I always assumed that for something like this to happen, there had to be a precise timing of each event. That's not exactly true. What you need is for each event to occur in order. As long as the events happen in order (1 – 2 – 3 – 4 & 5), that prophecy can be fulfilled. The time between events can be vastly different. That difference in timing can allow for the effects of free will. The time between any two events could be measured in minutes, days, months, years, etc. If you think of prophecies as relying on order more than timing, you eliminate any conflict between free will and prophecy.

I want to share a thought I have about prophecies. I believe that some prophecies are absolute and must happen. I think that other prophecies are more about what could happen rather than what will actually happen. An "absolute" prophecy must happen and can not be avoided because it is absolute. However, I feel a "warning" prophecy is there to make us aware of some possible future event. A warning prophecy may be avoidable. A lot will depend on choices that we make now. Unfortunately, I do not have a clue on how to tell the difference between "absolute" or "warning" prophecies. So how can you decide which prophecies are which? I guess my best advice would be to not to worry about it. Many of these prophecies talk about the "end" time. There are many religious books that say we will not know when the "end" is coming. I believe that is much more right than wrong. If you can find your faith, then you do not need to know when the end is coming. When a person has found their faith, they can use that to get through a lot of situations. People talk about getting their "house in order" for their end time. Why not keep your house in order all the time? If the end does come, you will be ready. So I try to plan for tomorrow but always <u>live</u> for today. Keeping your life in order every day can help to make your life more peaceful and enjoyable. Those are good things to have!

Fears

I want to talk a little about fears. All of us have fears. Some of these fears we will carry with us all of our lives and other fears we will be able to get past. This is part of being human. I have had friends that had terrible fears of spiders, mice and other things. I do not like things like spiders, bugs, rodents, etc. but I am not terrified of these things. However, the fears that people have are very real and should be respected.

Where I am going with this is not to diminish the reality of a person's fears but to tell you about the greatest fears in my life right now. In the past, I have faced off against a level 3 demon. A regular demon is bad enough but a level 3 demon is so much worse. I never want to encounter such a demon again but I can say I don't tremble in fear at that thought. The importance of addressing your fears is that fears can weigh our soul down. The more we can lessen the impact of fears on our lives, the more we can enjoy life. We may never be able to eliminate fears from our lives. The following are the two particular things that I am most fearful about.

The first fear isn't really a fear of dying but a fear of dying before my wife. I don't want to die quite yet but as long as I am here, I want to take the best care of my wife that I can. Remember that my wife is invalid. I have seen how she was cared for in a rehab situation and it was not good. I worry about what type of care my wonderful wife would get if I should pass before her.

The other fear that I have is that I will have to call an ambulance to take me or my wife to a local emergency room. We have not had good luck there. But before I go any farther I need to tell you this note. In January, 2019, my wife had to go to the local ER and was admitted to the local hospital for two days. The Angels did what they said they would do and everything worked out well. Knowing this decreases my fear about going to the ER but I will be honest and say that it does not eliminate my fear. I am human and sometimes it can be very hard to go beyond the past. It is better for us if we can get past things like this but it's not easy.

In 1981, I fell at home and broke my neck. I've already told you this story. If my wife would not have insisted that the doctor call a radiologist back in, the doctor would have sent me home and I would have likely been dead before Monday. The next event happened in the early 1990's. My dad called me in a panic. He had taken my mom to the ER because she was losing feeling in one leg but they had sent her home. He was home with her now. She was not able to get out of the car and she was getting worse. I asked who the doctor was. I told my father to take her back to the ER. I called the doctor. I wanted to know how the doctor could release somebody to go home that was obviously having a stroke. My mother was admitted after they got back to the hospital. She then spent over two months in rehab before she was strong enough to come home. She never was able to drive again after the stroke but she taught herself how to write again. When I would visit my parents, my mother had several pads of paper filled with writing. She spent many months practicing but she did write again.

My wife became ill with GBS in 2008. She came home after having many weeks of rehab at the hospital. The hospital then recommended outpatient rehab at their local facility. They let her fall three times at this rehab. One time, she tore open her leg. She still has scars on that leg to this day. In 2014, my wife was admitted to the local hospital for about two weeks with double pneumonia. This left her extremely weak. Before she got pneumonia, she could walk around the house with assistance. I could take her out to shop and other things by using a wheelchair. When the hospital was ready to discharge her, they talked her into going to one of their rehab units. When I got to the hospital that day, they had already got her to sign all the paperwork. This was all done without letting me be involved. At that time, she was on lots of pain medications. She doesn't remember signing any of that paperwork for rehab. The stay at rehab was supposed to be for two to four weeks. It turned into me taking her out of the rehab facility after 12 weeks with my wife in worse condition that when she went into it. They kept her drugged up so that she does not remember much of the first four or more weeks of rehab. Doctors were rarely available to talk to. Because of her GBS, she needs help eating but they usually did not have enough time to help her. Many days, she did not get fed much until I got there.

I was at rehab every day after work and at least twice a day on my days off to take care of her. They let her fall a couple of times so they restricted her to a Hoyer sling lift. A couple of days before I took her out of there, they flipped the Hoyer lift over with her in it. That happened in the morning. I called rehab on my lunch break to check on my wife. They said that she was fine. It wasn't until I got to rehab that evening that I found out what had happened. One side of her face was swollen and bruised. They had lied to me about her and what had happened. I got her out of there within a couple of days after that incident. But just before I rescued her from that facility, a nurse flagged me as I was leaving one evening. There were cameras all over so the nurse kept looking down at her medical cart. Her head still looking down, she whispered to me "get her (my wife) out of here before we kill her." Then, in a normal voice, she looked at me, said "have a good night" and went about her rounds. I got my wife out of that place a couple of days later.

We had the worst experience with the ER in 2015. I told you this story earlier - the ER experience. This is why one of my fears is that me or my wife will have to go to an ER or hospital. We have had several bad experiences there.

I talked to you about Angelic gatherings earlier. Because I have written this book, the Angels have told me that if my dear wife or I ever have to go to the ER or hospital, they (the Angels) will be there in mass. The Angels said: **there won't even be standing room.** A warning to all the medical staff! A gathering of Angels like this can make an atheist weak in the knees. This type of gathering offer makes me feel much better, but I am human and can not help having concerns about my wife's care.

Since writing this section about fears, my wife did have to go back to the ER and she spent two days in the hospital in January of 2019. As I said earlier, everything turned out well. She had excellent care this time. She was cared for by what is one of the best doctors I have ever had the opportunity to meet. The Angels had said they would do and the hospital was completely inundated with Angels. My Angels have never let me down. They told me that if either of us went to the hospital, the Angels would be there in mass. And they were there in MASS! 15 to 20 THOUSAND Angels in one place is a lot. The hospital was overflowing with Angels. This is where I saw many people stop in the halls and just look around. They KNEW that something was different but they just could not figure out what was different. It was quite a gathering of Angels. Most people are not likely to ever encounter that many Angels in one place during their lifetime.

I never questioned whether the Angels would come. But I am human and that can make me have doubts, sometimes when I should not have doubts. To my Angels: I will try harder to never have any doubts about anything I am told by you.

Forgiveness

We are human. A part of being human means that we are imperfect. We want God to forgive us for our mistakes. And God will give us a path to get forgiveness. We need to find a way here on Earth to find forgiveness for those that have wronged us. This isn't easy for most of us to do. When someone does something to you that is hurtful, it can be very difficult to go past that hurt. This is especially true if the hurt has a physical nature. It is always easier to forgive a person if we can distance ourselves from that person. But we don't always have that choice. So what can we do? You will have to find your own answer to that question. Each person will have their own individual answer.

There are many people in this world that do not think twice about using, misusing, abusing and in general taking advantage of someone. People like these are hypocritical in their attitudes and a big pain in our sides. We all get to deal with people like these at some time. It could be a boss, a neighbor, a family member or sometimes even a friend. I have definitely had all of these. If we let them, these people can do damage to us and can ruin our lives. We do not need to let this happen. Ultimately, we all will pay a price for our actions. These people will have to pay a much bigger price for their actions.

The best path I have found is forgiveness. If you can, get away from these people and keep them out of your life. That makes it easier. But you need to find forgiveness in your heart. The hurt and anger that they have caused you can be like a poison. This is a bad poison that eats at your very soul. We might not be able to forgive these people right away.   But it is important that we work hard to forgive them for the wellness of our own being. Forgiveness does not mean that you have to like or ever want to be around these people. Forgiveness should mean that you wish them no harm or ill will.

There are people that say you should forgive and forget. The forgive part of this is absolutely correct. That is your best course for you to have a better life. The forget part is an entirely different thing. There will be times when forgive and forget could be your best path. There will be other times that forget will never work. If somebody wronged you enough, you may not be able to forget it especially if that person has not changed at all. If that person has changed, then they might not wrong you again. There are a couple of sayings I'm going to use here. "A skunk can't change it's stripe" and "A leopard can't change it's spots." What I'm saying here is that a person may say that they have changed but it is often very hard for a person to change their true nature. Use caution with these people. That will be your best course. If we forget the past, we are doomed to repeat it. Unfortunately, that applies to both the world and the individual.

This is a story that relates to forgiveness. This story happened many years ago. It goes like this. Several veterans were in a cafe chatting. It turns out that two of them had been POW s during the war. They both had been treated badly by the enemy as POW s. The first guy asked the other guy if he had forgiven his enemy captors. The other guy answered: "No and I will never forgive them!" The first guy replies to him: "Then they still have you prisoner." Please don't be a prisoner.

Faith

Faith can mean many different things to different people. I only intend to tell you what faith has come to mean to me. It is your job to figure out how faith fits into your life. I sincerely hope that you do figure out how to have faith in your life. Even if you can't see it right now, faith is a critical issue in a person's life. Finding faith in your life is supremely important for you now and for your future.

There were definitely times in my life that my faith was weak. There was even a time earlier in my life that I might have said that I was an atheist. Boy, did I have that wrong! Many people with great minds have focused their lives on what is rational and factual but have ended up seeing that there is so much to this world that there has to be a Supreme Power. Life is <u>not</u> an accident. Life is intentional. The exact order of events that gave us life is not as important as the fact that we are here right now and alive. Why are we alive? Because of the actions of a Supreme Being. This is where faith comes into my picture of life. We are the result of the actions of God. We are promised much more after this physical life. This can help you to to find your faith. Our Supreme Being and all the Angels are real. If you take the time to look around you and look closely, you can see that all this place we call Earth is rich with life. That life is an orchestrated event - not some accident. Your faith should reside in your heart. That is part of why we have a heart. So that it can be a home for our faith. Everyone has the capacity to find their own faith within themselves. Remember, your heart is a part of your soul.

I have already told you this but I'm going to repeat it. When my Angels asked me to write about them, I felt totally overwhelmed by that idea. I asked myself: "Who am I to write a book about Angels?" When I did start writing, I was struggling to find words that felt "right." Late one night (February 13, 2018), I was sitting at the computer, totally frustrated. I mumbled: "How am I supposed to write a book about Angels?" The Angel to my left answered: **You already know what to write. Just look to your heart.** My point is that there is a foundation for our faith that we are born with. It is already there within your soul. We just must decide to build on it.

The definition of faith implies that you either have it or you don't. However, most people talk about faith in a scaled way. Often, people will say someone has little faith or someone else might have a lot of faith. If you can measure faith, then can a person have absolute faith? I say yes. Absolute faith would be faith so strong that nothing – repeat – nothing can shake your faith. Can you have absolute faith? I believe you can. Absolute faith can give a person a connection to God that is truly wonderful and beyond measure. May you find your faith!

Heaven

Heaven is the Kingdom of God. Heaven is where we want to eventually go to. I hope most people think that way. Now, is there a Hell? I think that certain people have lead very bad lives and they will need to do a lot of atonement to get into Heaven. Many of these people may be facing pathways through the Zone of Redress that are so difficult that these paths could easily look like Hell. That is what I think Hell is. Bad people will have to pay for their actions. Now, let's get back to Heaven. From what has been implied to me, Heaven is a really huge place. We are talking planet size only much larger than Earth. I have asked how many Angels there are. The best estimate I have for the number of Angels in Heaven is at least in the hundreds of trillions. And this estimate could very easily be to small. When I say there are a lot of Angels, I mean a lot. Just so you know, a trillion is a thousand billion or a million million. One hundred million looks like this: 100,000,000 and 100 trillion looks like this: 100,000,000,000,000. These are very large numbers!

We will all be offered a path to get to Heaven. It will be entirely up to each of us if we take that path. We will be completely different after we leave the Zone of Redress and are in Heaven. The impression that I have is that in Heaven we will be much more like Angels but still be ourselves. I do not have a better explanation than this right now. Angels are Angels and have always been Angles. People are people but we will change completely in Heaven and be different than we are here on Earth.

Since Heaven is the Kingdom of God, it is appropriate to talk about what God is all about. I'm not a scholar nor do I pretend to be. What I am is simply a person just like you. The only real difference is that for some reason, I have had the privilege to enjoy a lot of experiences with Angels. I have asked my Angels "why me" many times. Why am I able to see and communicate with Angels so much where most people aren't able to do this? I'm still waiting for a definitive answer to this question. However, my experiences have made me feel closer to God. Will all of us that get to Heaven meet God? I do not know. I don't even know if any of us will meet God. Different things that I've read state that there are multiple layers of Angels always surrounding God. I know that if God was to visit us here, we would not be able to face Him directly let alone understand His plan for us. But why is that necessary? God has provided us with as much information as we need. We will have the opportunity to grow and learn during our journey.

You and only you are responsible for your faith. Finding a religion that fits with your understanding can help your faith. Most religions share a common belief in the Supreme Being and His love for us. We always need to keep that as the focus of our faith. Some religions seem to lose some of this focus on certain words or phrases in their texts. If you always focus on God first, then every thing will eventually fall into place. It is your responsibility to find your own faith and make it work for you.

Do not lose focus of what the bigger meaning is in these books. And what is that? **LOVE**. Plain and simple, **LOVE**. More than anything else, I believe that God wants to be a loving and forgiving God. He has offered us pathways to His Kingdom. Let's use these pathways.

The Bible and other religious works are the greatest books in all of human history. Look at the core of all these books and you can see that they are talking about the same things. They have different words and stories but they still are all talking about the one Supreme Being and His love for us. You do not need to a religious scholar to understand what basic faith is all about. God made faith so that anyone who wants to have faith can find their faith. Faith is available to everyone.

We are human. I know I'm repeating myself here but it's important. We were born imperfect and still will be when we die. God can forgive us if we try to be good. We will err but we can learn from that and try not to repeat it. We should forgive others but there will be times that we will not be very successful at this.   It all comes back to love.   God gave us Angels to help us be better. Angels are an incredible tool in our lives. We should always try to let our Angels help us

This is not meant to be a sermon. I only want to share with you some of the things that Angels have shared with me. All of your life can be a chance to grow. When I look back at my life, I can see how different I am now compared with other parts of my life. Much of this change has come from growing and learning. I still have so much to learn. Never forget – Love. Love can replace so many bad things in our lives. I hope you think of love when you think of Heaven. That's what I think of. LOVE!

One last note. People have asked me if we will meet up with friends and relatives that have died before us. Angels have told me this: **We will be able to reconnect with loved ones** after we die. I'm taking that answer as a yes.

I hope you can accept these thoughts on Heaven. I'm not aware of any person that has actually been to Heaven and come back to give us a detailed description of Heaven. So I just tried to tell you what I believe is important to help you get there.   I hope we all have a good trip.

The End?

I had a beginning to this book. Does that mean I have to have an end? This book has truly been an unexpected journey. I knew this book would be hard to write. I would have to relive many very intense and personal moments to tell my story. It's been all that and so much more. I know I can write a book now. It will be up to the future to find out how well I was able to tell my story. I will repeat this one last time, my story. If you like the book, I'll say thank you very much. If you don't like this book, I will still say thank you. You gave me a chance. You may disagree with things that I have said here. That is okay with me. I only wanted to share some parts of my life with you. We are each on our own individual journeys. We will see the same things from many different angles. Our understanding of these things will be different because of this. But we will find that we share many common things. Angels are very real. God is absolutely real. As you know, you have free will and can deny all of this. Look around you. The truth is all around us.

Angels do things with a purpose. They don't mince words. I now realize so many events in my life where all leading up to me being able to write this book. You begin to see how things in your life connect when you look back on your journey. You see how one choice leads to another and yet another. This continued on to get me to where I'm at right now. It is so hard to see these things as you are going through them. What is that old saying: "hindsight is always 20/20 vision."

Something in this book is important to all the other Angels that have joined in on this. I often had three or more Angels around me during my life. At times, there would be groups with hundreds of Angels around. I thought that was great. Then came the day that they asked me to write a book about Angels. The exact words are: **You should write a book about us (Angels)**. That's when more Angels showed up. I thought that they had just shown up when I was asked to write this book. I was wrong. The Angels all stayed. The idea of this book felt like such a monumental task. Many days went by and all the Angels were still here. There were at least several hundred Angels around every day. I was not used to that many Angels around. I said to myself maybe I could try and write a book about Angels. They knew what I was thinking and more Angels came. Many, many more came. It took me a couple of weeks before I could convince myself that I might be able to write a book like this. The Angels waited for my decision. So the night came that I had decided. I was in the kitchen. There was a crowd of Angels present. I looked at all of the Angels and said: "Okay, I'll write a book about you (Angels)." They raised their arms and all yelled: **Yeah! Yeah! Yeah!**. I was shocked! Whenever I went somewhere after that night, all the open fields around us were filled with Angels looking at me. All the Angels would be smiling. We are talking big fields filled with Angels. I really was wondering what I had gotten myself in to.

This mass of Angels continued until I actually started the book. Then it changed. New Angels showed up: the Scholar Angels. Most of the other Angels backed away but stayed. There has been a ring of Angels around me and my house since then. The Angels are just standing shoulder to shoulder in a giant ring. They are still there tonight as I am continuing to write this book. I have gotten used to this many Angels around. It is quite nice to have all these Angels close. I guess my next question is: what happens when the book is done? Will most of the Angels leave? Will the "heart" on my side go away? I will find out seen enough.

How do I follow this book if it becomes successful? I have an idea. I now have a website. I could set up the web site to accept questions. I might be able to answer some of these questions. If there is a followup book, it could have a question - answer theme to it. It would still be "My Life with Angels" but with more interaction with the reader. It would be worth it if it could help people understand Angels better. I'll have to wait and see. I don't think I've got to that page in my **Book of Life** yet.

What do I need to say yet? What more should I try to tell you now? I doubted that I could write this book. My Angels never doubted me. We should have love in our life and try very hard to be happy. God loves us more than most of us know. We need to love Him back. Our future will offer us many incredible things.

Just a last update. The day that I declared this book done was February 14, 2019. The book was written but far from being ready to be published. That day a lot of Angels showed up in support of my efforts. A lot of Angels. That day I saw more Angels than at any other time in my life. It was incredible and completely overwhelming. Those Angels were mostly gone the next day. It is back to normal now. Sort of. I guess I should ask what my normal is?

Angels do things with a purpose. I doubt that we would understand the things that Angels do even if we knew the reasons behind their actions. Angels are always near us. Someday you may get to see an Angel. It could happen. Someone once asked me if more Angels will be seen after this book is out there. I looked at the Angels around us at that moment. The Angels all had what I call "Mona Lisa" type smiles. They shrugged their shoulders at that question. I will leave it up to you how to interpret that answer. It is not the first time and probably not the last time I will get an answer like that from Angels.

One last time – Thank you. Gary

WHY ME?

I said that I would try to tell you why I think I have been able to see and "talk" to Angels all my life. I have always wondered about this. That is the question: "Why me?" When I was talking to someone about the book, the "why me?" question came up. The person thought a moment and came back with a potential answer: "Why not you." I had to think about that answer. It was as good an answer as any other answer. A person does not have to be someone special to have an Angelic encounter. However, that answer still didn't feel like it was complete. You can ask an Angel anything but that Angel will only answers some of the questions. I'm at the editing stage of the book when the Angels give me a possible answer to the "why me" question. This is an answer that I have never even considered. I will need some time to ponder this answer.

I need to start by reminding you about when I was born. The year was 1951 and I was born "sick." My mother told me that many times. I was only given a 50/50 chance of living for the first two days of my life. They told my parents they had done everything that they could and only time would tell. If I could make it through those first two days, my chances of living would improve each day.

Medical technology was very different in 1951 than it is today. About the best that doctors could do in a situation like mine was to give me a shot, likely penicillin, and put me in a controlled environment like an incubator. They did not have all the monitoring systems that are used today. Monitoring a patient at that time would have been done by a person, most likely a nurse, who would actually watch that patient. The hospital that I was born in was closed many years ago and has since been torn down.

What the Angels told me was this: **<u>You died the first day of your life but were brought back</u>**. They said that I had actually died for 27 minutes. The Angels showed me an image of one clock that read 3:17. Then a second clock that read 3:44. That is how I got the 27 minutes. I questioned the Angels: "27 minutes?" The Angels all nodded. The impression that I have is that this happened in the middle of the night. The Angels said that this happened during the first day (24 hours) of my life. I don't think that anybody at the hospital even knew that this happened. If they did know, how could they explain me dying and coming back? I was in the hospital several more weeks before my parents could bring me home. I believe that this happened in the middle of the night and nobody knew about it. I only have what the Angels have told me to support this.

The bottom line here is that I was given a second chance at life. When someone dies, there are many Angels involved. If I was dead that many minutes, there is a great chance that I would have encountered many different Angels during that period. Those Angelic encounters could be part of why I have always had close connections to Angels. When I look at my life, this answer to "why me" seems to create the best picture yet for my life. It feels the most right of any answer. So far -

What happened to me is part of my journey. Each of us is on our own journey and your experiences will be different from mine. Is the event that I had when I was born the entire reason I can interact with Angels?   I do feel that the experience is significant and could be part of my Angel experiences. Someday, I might get a complete answer to the "why me" question. Or maybe not.

The thought of getting a second chance has come as quite a revelation to me. It is both wonderful and overwhelming to think that you were given a second chance. There's one last thing that I must say. To the Powers that Be: thank you – thank you – thank you. This is truly more of "an unexpected journey" than I ever imagined!

P.S. The Angels waited to tell me about my second chance experience until after I had this book written but not finished it. I have no idea why they did it this way. Maybe, someday, I will find this out – or maybe not. Once again, who knows?

The Most Unusual

These two events are the most private and personal of all my experiences to date. I thought long and hard as to whether I should include them. Ultimately, I have decided to include them because they are a significant part of my life and this book. These events will challenge your ability to believe my experiences much more than any of the other experiences that I have told you about. But they are as real as all the other experiences. With that said, here goes -

The "Heart"

This is about one of the most unusual experiences I have had with Angels. I have asked the Angels about this event many times. I get smiles from them when I ask about this but never an answer. It does involve a "heart" or should I say the image of a heart.

This event happened in early June, 2014. My wife was in a rehab facility at this time so I was at home alone. I had to be up early for work the next day so I had went to bed early. My normal sleep ware are boxers and a t-shirt. It was extra warm in the house that night so I had taken off my t-shirt. I finally went to sleep.

Later, I am startled awake by Angels. The room was completely overflowing with Angels. Angels were everywhere. Angels were even floating above me. Angels do not normally appear like this. This was the first time I have ever had them surround me this way. The really odd thing about all this was that the Angels were all grinning. I've seen Angels smile many times. It's just not that common for them to grin like this. I was just looking at them. Then an Angel directly above me says: **You can go back to sleep now.** Why did they wake me up and then tell me to go back to sleep? That is all I could think of at that moment. Let it be known that if an Angel says you can go to sleep now, guess what? You go to sleep! You don't think about sleeping. You calmly and peacefully go to sleep. I did go back to sleep and slept until the alarm went off.

Morning is here now. I started getting ready for work. All that I could think about was how strange that Angelic encounter had been. A bunch of Angels had woke me up to say go back to sleep? It was not making any sense. I did remember having an incredible dream just when they woke me up. The dream made me feel like I was floating in some vast space almost like the sky with blue and purple streaks of color. I was feeling a level of calmness and peacefulness that was amazing. Yet at the same time, I felt filled with this wonderful energy. There were many, many Angles moving around in the dream. It is very hard to describe. If you haven't noticed by now, it can be very hard to find words to describe an Angelic encounter. Most words lack the intensity that an Angelic encounter has. This encounter was much more powerful than most.

As I'm taking a shower before work, I notice what looks like a mark on my right side. It didn't hurt or itch so I didn't pay much attention to it right then. I needed to focus on getting ready and going to work. I would end up thinking about the Angels and the dream all day long. I hurried home after work, changed clothes and headed off to rehab to be with my wife for the rest of the day. I get home later and I'm getting ready for bed when I remember the mark on my side. I should check this out. It wasn't uncommon to get a bruise from handling cases of product at work. I look at the mark on my side. It is not a bruise or a rash. It is a red mark shaped like a heart. It is shaped just like a classic Valentine heart. It does not hurt and it's not tender or sore. It is flat with the rest of the skin around it. It's about two inches wide and two inches high. I'm thinking what is this? Then I remember the dream and the Angels the previous night. I look to the Angels that are all around me. I ask them what is the "heart" all about. All I get from them are grins. And these are very big grins. The Angels are not saying anything. That did not surprise me. Angels will only tell you things when you need to know things. I'm thinking that my Guardian Angels had "given" me the heart because the only Angels that I saw the night before were Guardian Angels. But they would not tell me anything.

Life goes on and several years later my Angels ask me to write this book. I always have taken the subject of Angels very seriously. As I have said before, I honestly had to think a lot about writing this book. So I start the book. Then the icicle cross appears on the eave on February 13, 2018. I find out that the icicle cross was not put on the eave by my Guardian Angels. There is a special Angel that leaves signs and messages for people. That would be a Message Angel. Then it finally made sense. Guardian Angels can touch you but they will not leave any marks on you. However, A Message Angel can leave a mark or sign on a person. That's their job. What I thought was a dream was not a dream at all. I was experiencing the touch of a Message Angel. That is also what woke me up and why the other Angel said to go back to sleep. The "heart" had been delivered.

I still do not know the significance of the "heart". It was given to me in 2013. It's always had a sharply defined edge. I took the photo of the heart in March, 2018. That is the photo of the "heart" in this book. The heart developed a notch on one side late in the summer of 2018. It changed more in the summer of 2019. The edge on one side changed shape some. These changes happened over night. I still do not have any idea why I have this "heart" or its meaning. But the "heart" is still there. Slightly changed but still there. I think the next question is will the heart change more next year? I'll find out next year.

There is one thing I find disconcerting about the heart. Why did a Message Angel pick that location? The location never concerned me until I saw a show on the Shroud of Turin. A part of the show was describing were blood stains where on the shroud. While Christ was on the cross, a Roman soldier pierced his right side. The shroud shows blood stains on the right side of where the body was wrapped. These blood stains are around ribs T-4 and T-5. The "heart" is by my ribs T-4 and T-5 on my right side. Why was the "heart" put at that spot? What does all this mean? I still don't know.

P.S. If you read this book and we met, please don't ask me to take my shirt off. Why? I'm in my late sixties and could lose a few pounds. Enough said. Thank you.

The Visit

There have been many sections in this book that have been very personal and hard to write about. In many ways, this is the hardest part of book to write. This is by far the most <u>intense</u> Angelic encounter of my entire life. I have only now shared it with my wife since I started writing this book. I still wonder about whether it should be include in the book.

Let me start by reminding you that everything in this book actually happened. It's understandable if you find some of the experiences in this book difficult to believable. I need to remind you that they all really happened. Even to this very day, I find this event to be both incredible and amazing. It was real and it did happen. I've always heard that fact is harder to believe than fiction. So here we go...

This happened in 1979. Both my wife and I worked night shifts at this time. My wife was working that night and I had that night off. I had gone to bed and was sound asleep. There was suddenly this blinding light in the bedroom. The light woke me up and I sat up in bed. What I woke up to was totally breathtaking!

There where Angels everywhere. I had never experienced any Angels like these before. There were many small Cherub like Angels near the ceiling and in every corner of the room. There where six feminine Angels with wings, three to each side of the bed. They were floating past the end of the bed. Beyond the end of the bed where many rows of Soldier Angels. There where several types of Soldier Angels. They were all in rows. But that was not all. There where two Angels at the end of the bed. The Angel to the left was at least 7 feet tall. He was wearing military attire including a helmet. His outfit was completely different than the other Angels. The Angel to the right was shorter, less than 6 feet tall, wearing a long robe and had shoulder length brown hair. All the Angels are looking at me now. Not just looking, but staring at me. I know my mouth was probably open. When I remember this, I usually open my mouth without thinking about it. It's just a reaction to the memory of this event.

Then it happens. The Angel on the left speaks! He says: **Do not be afraid. I am Archangel Micheal. We are here to read to you from your 'Book of Life'. It will tell you your future**. What? I have an Archangel in the room with all his entourage. I am very much in shock. I then notice that the Angel to the right has a large book under his right arm. He proceeds to lift the book up and in front of him. A lectern appears and he puts the book on top of it. He opens the book up. All the Angels, including Micheal, are now looking at the that Angel. He looks at me. He looks down to the book and starts to read. His voice is very calming and comforting. He turns the pages and reads on.

It felt like this went on for a long time but I do not really know. Then, the second Angel stops reading. He looks at me, smiling and closes the book. All of the Angels are smiling and looking at me. Micheal is looking at me and smiling. Then, Micheal speaks: **You now know the rest of your life. You will only remember your future as you need to.** There is a slight pause and then Micheal speaks again: **You can go to sleep now.** As I said before, when an Angel says go to sleep to you, you sleep. And I was out for the rest of the night. I woke up when Steph got home in the morning. She was tired and went right to bed. I stayed in bed for a while. Thinking and pondering.

I wanted to tell myself that the event had never happened. The entire experience was just a very strange dream. No matter how hard I tried to convince myself that it was only a "dream", it was useless. I knew what had happened was real. Like I said earlier, I chose not to share this with anyone until now. And that is only because of this book. I have revisited that night many times. Likewise, it has also revisited me many times. As life has gone on, that night comes back to me when I reach certain events in my life. I'll only remember things from that night as I needed to know them. And that is exactly the way it has happened.

I think you can probably understand my reservations about including this event in the book. Me, having a visit from Archangel Micheal? It really happened. Even today this experience is still overwhelming and makes me feel slightly numb if I think about it. I'm choosing to leave this story as is. The story is complete enough. I have left out a few details. Maybe I will talk more about this experience someday. Or maybe not. There are some things that are best kept personal and private. Especially when it comes to Angels. Yes, I was visited by Archangel Micheal! WOW!

I don't know how long my "Book of Life" is. It makes me wonder how long I will have on this Earth. I just know that occasionally, I find out more about my journey. We don't really need to know how long we will be on this Earth. We should just keep going. What's that saying? Plan for tomorrow but <u>always</u> live for today. I like that thought.

I tell you many things about my life in various sections of this book so I'm not going into much biographical information on this page. I was born in southwestern lower Michigan and have lived there all my life. I have not traveled much in my life. My wife did a lot of traveling for a job she had and was able to get us to Paris twice. Even though we where in Paris for only a couple of days each time, we made that time as memorable as possible. The photo on this page is of myself in front of a house that Van Gogh once lived in. My wife likes this photo so this is what I picked to include on this page. The photo was taken about 20 years ago. I definitely look older now. As I told you earlier in the book, I have an avid interested in creative things including painting. That is one of the reasons my wife wanted to get me to Paris, to see some great museums and their art. I did buy a wood folding easel in Paris. Carrying that easel around Paris and getting that easel home is a story of its own.

This is a photo of the heart on my side. The heart was left there by an Angel. The heart is about 2 inches by 2 inches. This photo was taken at a slight angle. The heart is very symmetrical. I have had it since June of 2014. I don't know why it was given to me. I only know that it was given to me by a Message Angel. I have asked why I have this heart many times and have never gotten an answer.

The heart remained unchanged until July of 2018. The heart developed a notch on the inside edge. It remained unchanged until July of 2019. Some of the out side edge has changed shape a little and is less curved. All these changes happened over night. I still have no idea why any of this has happened. I have asked the Angels many times about the "heart." The only response I ever get when I ask the Angels is that they will all grin at me. After having the "heart" change two years in a row, is it going to change more. I do wonder is the "heart" will go away when I complete the book. Some days the heart is redder and other days the heart is much paler. I can't explain that either. Who know?

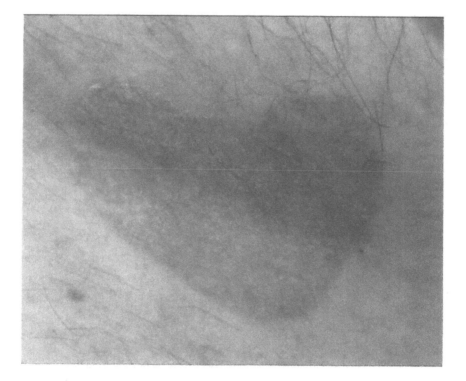

CPSIA information can be obtained
at www.ICGtesting.com
Printed in the USA
JSHW020750151219
2955JS00001B/1